PROGRESS & RELIGION

CHRISTOPHER DAWSON

PROGRESS
AND
RELIGION

AN HISTORICAL ENQUIRY

GREENWOOD PRESS, PUBLISHERS
WESTPORT, CONNECTICUT

Originally published in 1929
by Sheed and Ward, London

First Greenwood Reprinting 1970

Library of Congress Catalogue Card Number 79-104266

SBN 8371-3917-1

Printed in the United States of America

To
MY PARENTS

PREFACE

THE doctrine of Progress was first clearly formulated by the Abbé de St. Pierre after the close of the War of the Spanish Succession, at a time when he was conducting his propaganda for the formation of a kind of League of Nations which should ensure perpetual peace in Europe. For two centuries it has dominated the European mind to such an extent that any attempt to question it was regarded as a paradox or a heresy, and it is only during the last twenty years that its supremacy has begun to be seriously challenged. By a curious irony of circumstance, the years which have seen the partial fulfilment of the Abbé's hopes have also witnessed the disappearance of that unquestioning faith in social progress of which he was the protagonist.

It is easy to understand the immediate causes of this change. The accumulated strain and suffering of four years of war ended either in defeat and revolution, or in victory and disillusion, and it was natural enough that, in such circumstances, there should be a tendency to despair of the future of Europe, and to take refuge in fatalistic theories of the inevitability of cultural decline.

But behind this temporary movement of discouragement and disillusion there are signs of a deeper change, which marks the passing, not merely of an age or a social order, but of an intellectual tradition. We are accustomed to speak of this change as a reaction from Victorian ideas, but something much more fundamental is at stake, for Victorian ideas were but the English middle-class version of the optimistic Liberal creed, which had set out to re-fashion the world in the preceding century.

This creed has played somewhat the same part in our civilization as that taken by religion at other periods of history. Every living culture must possess some spiritual dynamic, which provides the energy necessary for that sustained social effort which is civilization. Normally this dynamic is supplied by a religion, but in exceptional circumstances the religious impulse may disguise itself under philosophical or political forms.

It is this vital relation between religion and culture which I have attempted to study in the present book. Sociologists in the past have tended to disregard or minimize the social functions of religion, while students of religion have concentrated their attention on the psychological or ethical aspects of their subject. If it is true, as I believe, that every culturally vital society must possess a religion, whether explicit or disguised, and that the religion of a society determines to a great extent its cultural form, it is obvious that the whole problem of social development and change must be studied anew in relation to the religious factor. I cannot hope to have succeeded in doing this in the limits of the present essay, but it is enough if I have at least suggested the possibilities of a new way of approach.

I must express my thanks to the editors and publishers of the *Sociological*, the *Quarterly*, and the *Dublin Reviews*, for allowing me to make use of some passages from articles which have appeared in these reviews at various times during the last ten years. I must also gratefully acknowledge the help of my friend, Mr. E. I. Watkin, who has been kind enough to read the proofs and to prepare the list of contents.

CONTENTS

CHAPTER I

The idea of Progress has been the inspiration of the modern civilization of Western Europe. Its empirical justification. The development of machinery and applied science has produced an industrial-scientific civilization unique in the world's history. Its value is now widely criticized. 18th century self-confidence—the offspring of Renaissance culture and Cartesian Rationalism. A secularist apocalyptic. *Ratio liberata facit omnia nova.* The 19th century inherits the rationalist faith of the Aufklärung. Comte's positivism. Dominance of scientific materialism. Herbert Spencer. Human progress and reason bye-products of a blind cosmic evolution. Pessimism. Huxley and Bertrand Russell. Anti-intellectualist reaction. Pragmatism. Vitalism. Persistance of belief in progress and in industrial-scientific civilization.

CHAPTER II.

Rise of the historical school in Germany. German ideal intuition not discursive reason. Opposition to mechanist science. A musical not a mathematical interpretation of life. Valuation of history and nationality. The Nation as a spiritual unit. Discovery of the Middle Ages. Hegelian philosophy of history and the state. History the progressive manifestation of Absolute Spirit. Nationalist bias of history in the 19th century. Rise of comparative history of cultures. The life-cycle of a culture —analogous phases. " Predetermination of history." Western culture in its final stage—civilization—cosmopolitan, positive, imperial—the analogue of the Roman

ix

CHAPTER III

CONTENTS

CHAPTER IV

Despite the importance of environment cultures are mal-
leable by thought and invention. From the first man has
been an artist and a conqueror of nature, e.g., the palæolithic cave artists. The outlook of the primitive not confined to his physical needs, e.g., the elaborate religious
ceremonial of the Australian tribes. The inner aspect of
a culture the most important and distinctive. Every culture
possesses a distinctive view of life—its soul and formative
principle. Behind every civilization is a vision collective
or individual. Cultures chiefly differentiated and changed
by intellectual or spiritual factors—not however always or
chiefly by scientific knowledge or rational criticism. Religion
—a sense of dependence on superhuman powers—the womb
of civilization. Primitive religion universal and vague.
Matter the reflection and outward manifestation of spiritual
beings. Belief in an indefinite supernatural power diffused
throughout nature—Orenda, Wakan. An " ocean of supernatural energy." Mythology distinct from religion—and to
the primitive himself unimportant. It is a crude speculation which often contaminates and weakens religion. Profound religious experience of primitives which often verges
on mysticism.

CHAPTER V

The sociology of the 18th and 19th centuries blind to the
importance of religion as a cultural factor. The secularism
of modern civilization abnormal and transitory. Its divorce
between the inner and outer aspects of human life fatal
to its permanence. The primitive cultures are *religion
cultures*. Religion intervenes in every human activity and
the most important member of society is the man who
mediates between the supernatural powers and his fellows—
the Medicine Man, the Shaman. Religious initiation among
the North American Indians. Inherited magical technique.
Magic the cradle of science—itself the product of distinctively

xi

CHAPTER VII

CONTENTS

of Latin Christianity. Dynamic and social theology of
St. Augustine. The City of God. Man's will God's instrument to create a new world. Civilizing work of the Papacy
and Benedictine monasticism. Mediæval, civilization a
creation of the Church based on ecclesiastical, not civil
unity. Mediæval Europe a loose federation of diverse races
and cultures under the hegemony of a common religion.
Europe tended to become a theocratic church state.
Secularization of the Church prevented by the spiritual
revival of 12th and 13th centuries. Devotion to the Divine
Humanity. The Franciscan ideal and the sanctification of
nature—Canticle of the Sun. The beginning of a new
humanism expressed in art and the democratic movements of
the 14th century. New intellectual synthesis. The Church
and the Aristotelian tradition. Scholasticism rationalist and
scientific. It affirms the autonomous character of Reason
and the importance of sensible experience. Nevertheless
St. Thomas' ideal was an absolute intellectualism, and he
could not foresee the possibility of a new physical science.
Hence the transitory character of the 13th century synthesis.
The nominalist reaction. The later Middle Ages a period of
disintegration. Birth of Nationalism and Secularism.

CHAPTER VIII

THE SECULARIZATION OF WESTERN CULTURE AND THE RISE
OF THE RELIGION OF PROGRESS 177

Rise of independent national cultures. Centrifugal movement. The Italian Renaissance the reassertion of Latin
culture. The Reformation, the assertion of cultural independence by Northern Europe. Frontiers between Protestant
and Catholic Europe mainly coincident with the frontiers of
the Roman Empire. Luther led and impersonated the revolt
of the simple Teutonic against the complex Latin tradition.
Lutheranism " a spiritual Peasant revolt." Rejection of
Hellenic element in Christianity. Protestantism a religion
of world affirmation and practical action. But secular
progress was born not of Protestantism but of the Renaissance
culture of Latin Europe—itself also a secularization of
human life. The Renaissance predominantly æsthetic—life

xiv

CONTENTS

as a fine art. Art and the scientific observation of nature.
Leonardo da Vinci. Influence of Platonism. Modern
science the child of a marriage between the artistic genius
of the Renaissance and the mathematical idealism of the
Platonists. The new synthesis partial and mechanical. The
philosophic dualism of Cartesianism reflects a cultural
dualism. Religion and secular culture disparate and
hostile. But society as a whole remained under the dominion
of religious belief—now, however, a source of disunion.
Rise of secularist toleration. The Revolution of 1688.
The unity of European culture re-established on the basis
of international science. A universal religion of pure
reason. 18th century Deism, " the ghost of Christianity."
Belief in a future life replaced by belief in human perfectibility and indefinite progress. The Abbé de St. Pierre.
Belief in Progress the mainspring of French rationalism,
German idealism, and English Utilitarian Liberalism—also
of Rousseau's social idealism. Rousseau, the father of
the Revolution to which he gave the religious faith which it
sought to embody in a new social order. Reaction against
the Revolution—return to the Christian tradition. Opposition of Liberal Revolutionaries and Catholic Conservatives
in 19th century Europe. Rationalist Liberalism is a
secularized Catholicism, Rousseau's Revolutionary Idealism a secularized Apocalyptic. Apocalypticism of Godwin,
Shelley and the early Socialists. Religious interpretation
of Progress by the German philosophers. The idea of Progress fully developed and dominant in the first half of the
19th century.

CHAPTER IX

I

Industrial Revolution began in 18th century England.
English compromise with traditional Christianity. The
new science utilized by an industry fostered by the Protestant

CONTENTS

this-worldly asceticism of thrift and hard labour. Puritanism of the industrial middle class. Economic world conquest and exploitation. The world becomes a single community with an industrial-economic life and common
standards of material comfort. Political liberalism and
humanitarianism. Contemporary disillusionment. Social
discontent. Depressed condition of the worker—an irrespon-
sible cog in the machine. Socialism—a revolt against the new
social order and its ideals. Inherent instability of capitalist
industrialism. Europe losing her economic monopoly to the
danger of her political supremacy. Excessive urbanization
—consequent diminution of vitality and loss of contact with
nature. A warning from Roman history. If Europe falls,
civilization perishes. Need of social and moral unification.
Consolidation not revolution. Not Spartacus but Augustus.
Political and intellectual weakness of Liberalism. Progress
and perfectibility denied by the contemporary intelli-
gentsia. A religious basis and bond of European society
indispensable.

II

Since the 16th century Europe has suffered from intellectual
and spiritual disunion. Emancipated science has prospered
but philosophy has been banished. A mechanical explanation of reality leaves no room for moral and spiritual values.
The Deist compromise based on an act of irrational faith.
Conflict between science and metaphysics. Nineteenth
century triumph of mechanical determinism. No place for
progress or optimism. The struggle for existence. Reappear-
ance of the everlasting return. Nietzsche. The alternative
theory of the degradation of energy leading to final extinction of the universe. Science and Reality. Scientific law and
mathematical symbolism. Scientific knowledge limited
the quantitative aspects of reality. Science no substitute for
philosophy or religion. The Age of the Cinema—science in
the service of sensationalism. Social revolution as the product
of the repression of the religious impulse. Karl Marx. The
revolutionary attitude, common in the contemporary world,
the consequence of a divorce between religion and social life
fatal to civilization. Another warning from ancient Rome.
No religion, no culture.

xvi

CHAPTER X

PAGE

The culture of Western Europe the product of two factors (1) Judæo-Christian religion; (2) The scientific tradition derived ultimately from Greece. Neither indigenous. A rationalist and naturalist religion of science not intrinsically absurd. Wide demand for a neo-paganism which will possess the same attitude to nature as the primitive and archaic religions, while replacing ritual magic by scientific law. But man cannot worship the natural forces he conquers and exploits. Evolutionary vitalism. Bergson. Professor Alexander. Professor Julian Huxley. God the ideal emergent in man. Not purely scientific, not the obvious interpretation of the evolutionary process. Moral idealism of the West the fruit of traditional religion. The parting of the ways—Europe must abandon with Christianity her faith in progress and humanity or return to the religious foundation of her culture. The religion of Progress must be an historical religion—historic Christianity and the ideals of evolutionary vitalism. Philanthropy, social reform, scientific organization—all require the dynamic which Christianity provides. The progressive intellectualization of the material world by science must be co-ordinated with the progressive spiritualization of human nature by religion. This harmony has never been fully achieved though both factors have contributed to form European culture. Christianity and international unity. The ultimate ideal not a superstate, but a spiritual society.

PART I

I

SOCIOLOGY AND THE IDEA OF PROGRESS

E VERY period of civilization possesses certain characteristic ideas that are peculiarly its own. They express the mind of the society that has given them birth, no less than does the artistic style or the social institutions of the age. Yet so long as they are dominant, their unique and original character is never fully recognized, since they are accepted as principles of absolute truth and universal validity. They are looked on not as the popular ideas of the moment, but as eternal truths implanted in the very nature of things, and as self-evident in any kind of rational thinking.

Now the idea of Progress has occupied a position of this kind in the modern civilization of Western Europe. It has been far more than a philosophical opinion or the doctrine of a school, for it has permeated the whole mind of society from the leaders of thought down to the politicians and the men of business, who would be the first to proclaim their distrust of idealism and their hostility to abstract theorizing. It ha's been, in fact, the working faith of our civilization, and so completely has it become a part of the modern mind that any attempt to criticize it has seemed almost an act of impiety. Indeed nothing is more difficult than

3

to put oneself outside the age in which we live, and to make an impartial estimate of the fundamental ideas on which our civilization rests. For we are ourselves part of that which we are attempting to criticize, and we can no more separate ourselves from the all-pervading influence of our social and intellectual environment than the eye can separate itself from the light through which it receives all its impressions. If at the present day it is at last possible to trace the history of the idea of Progress and to understand the part that it has played in the development of modern civilization, it is to a great extent because that idea has begun to lose its hold on the mind of society and because the phase of civilization of which it was characteristic is already beginning to pass away. For in every department of life we are witnessing fundamental changes which seem to portend the close of that great epoch of civilization which embraced the 18th and 19th centuries, and the dawn of a new age.

Now the moment we begin to analyse the idea of Progress and to understand the consequences that it involves for social theory, we shall realize that it is by no means such a simple idea as we are apt to suppose.

The doctrine of Progress in the full sense must involve the belief that every day and in every way the world grows better and better. Yet the most enthusiastic supporters of the theory have been the very people who are most impatient of the injustice and irrationality of existing social institutions. And since the present state of the world is the result of a process that has endured for infinite ages, it would seem that the rate of progress is so slow that any

4

ultimate goal of perfection must lie in the infinitely distant future.

This, however, has not been the view of the believers in progress. The thinkers of the 18th and 19th centuries did not reckon in millions or even in thousands of years. On the contrary they had an optimistic faith in the abrupt advent of a new age of justice and enlightenment, in which their most extravagant hopes for the future of humanity would be realized. The belief in Progress found its chief support, not among the historians and anthropologists who traced the actual process of human development, but among the political theorists and revolutionaries whose whole attention was concentrated on the immediate future. And the same spirit reappears in the revolutionary political and socialist reformers of the 19th century, all of whom had an almost apocalyptic belief in the possibility of a complete transformation of human society—an abrupt passage from corruption to perfection, from darkness to light. Such a process is too sudden and catastrophic to be progressive, in fact what is known as the belief in Progress would often be more correctly described as the belief in human perfectibility.

If we turn from the theories of the social reformers and the doctrinaires to the opinions of the general public and the man in the street, the idea of Progress again changes its meaning. It denotes little more than a mental acceptance and a moral approval of that process of material and social change in the midst of which the modern man lives. It does not necessarily convey a belief in any vast process of gradual evolution. It is essentially bound up with that rapid improvement in the material conditions of existence which is a matter of daily experience. The idea of Progress hardly reached the masses until their lives had begun to be affected by the political changes of the revolutionary era on the continent, and in this country by the great economic changes of the last century.

At first the popular reaction to the latter was decidedly hostile and took the form of machine breaking and Luddite riots. Gradually, however, during the course of the century, men began to feel the benefits of the new order, and recognized that what was good enough for their fathers was no longer good enough for themselves. They adapted themselves whole-heartedly to the changes which they had not sought and for which they were not responsible. To-day, to the average European, and still more to the average American, Progress consists in the spread of the new urban-mechanical civilization : it means more cinemas, motor-cars for all, wireless installations, more elaborate methods of killing people, purchase on the hire system, preserved foods and picture papers.

It is easy enough to ridicule these naïve ideas— indeed they have been the stock-in-trade of the professional satirist for half a century and more. Yet perhaps they are fundamentally more justified than the more idealistic beliefs of the 18th century theorists. For it is impossible to deny that the last two centuries have witnessed the most rapid and remarkable changes in civilization that the world has ever known. Human existence has been transformed by the application of science to daily life and the mechanical control of the forces of nature.

6

A new industrial-scientific type of civilization, entirely unlike anything that has existed at any earlier period of the world's history, has made its appearance, and this has led to a vast increase in wealth and population and to the world-wide expansion of European culture. At the time of the Renaissance, Europe was still hard pressed by the forces of Islam, and the Mediterranean was in danger of becoming a Turkish lake. By the 19th century Europe had attained an undisputed world hegemony. The ancient civilizations of Asia were losing their independence and the resources of the New World and of the Antipodes were producing wealth for the European markets and food for the European populations. Moreover the changes in political and social organization were hardly less striking. All over Europe, and in the new lands of European culture across the seas, the old forms of government were giving place to democratic institutions. The rights of popular self-government and national self-determination and of the freedom of opinion were more completely realized than the most optimistic thinkers of earlier days could have deemed possible.

Finally, the great humanitarian movement has destroyed slavery and swept away the barbarous punishments which are almost as old as civilization, while the introduction of universal education has entirely transformed the intellectual life of the masses. Looked at from this point of view, Progress is no imaginary hypothesis but a solid reality of history.

But it is important to remember that this process of change is a strictly relative one. So far from being the necessary result of a universal process of evolution

7

which embraces the whole life of humanity, it is an exceptional and indeed unique achievement of a single society at a particular stage of its development. It is not necessarily more permanent than the other achievements of past ages and cultures. It may even be questioned, as indeed it has been questioned by many, whether the modern advance of material civilization is progressive in the true sense of the word; whether men are happier or wiser or better than they were in simpler states of society, and whether Birmingham or Chicago is to be preferred to mediæval Florence.

Nor are these doubts confined to prophets like Ruskin or Tolstoi, who preached a radical turning away from the victorious material civilization of the West and a return to the past, or a flight to the desert. Even those who fully accepted the scientific and material progress of the 19th century have come to realize the dangers and instability of the new order. They have felt the dangers of social parasitism and physical degeneration in the enormous and shapeless agglomerations of badly-housed humanity, which everywhere accompanied the progress of industrialism. They have seen the destruction of the finer forms of local life, and the disappearance of popular art and craftsmanship before a standardized mechanical civilization, as well as the havoc that has been wrought among the primitive peoples by European trade and conquest. They have realized the wastefulness of a system which recklessly exhausts the resources of nature for immediate gain, which destroys virgin forests to produce halfpenny newspapers, and dissipates the stored-up mineral energy of ages in an orgy of stench and smoke. To-day

8

few thinkers would be so bold as to identify the material advance of modern European civilization with Progress in the absolute sense, for we now realize that a civilization may prosper externally and grow daily larger and louder and richer and more self-confident, while at the same time it is decreasing in social vitality and losing its hold on its higher cultural traditions.

It has, however, taken us two centuries to reach this position. The men of the 18th century, who were the actual creators of the new movement of European culture, were troubled by no such doubts. They had a complete confidence in the absolute and universal validity of the principles on which they based their action. The dominant characteristic of the culture of the 18th century, which it had received as a direct heritage from the age of Louis XIV, was a conception of Civilization as something absolute and unique—a complete whole standing out in symmetrical perfection, like a classical temple against a background of Gothic confusion and Oriental barbarism. The same sentiment that Molière had expressed with regard to mediæval art :—

> Le fade goût des monuments gothiques,
> Ces monstres odieux des siècles ignorants,

—was shown towards all the social heritage of the past. Voltaire writes : " For 900 years the French genius has been almost always cramped under a Gothic government, in the midst of divisions and civil wars, without fixed laws or customs. . . . The nobles without discipline, knowing only war and idleness, churchmen living in disorder and ignorance, and the populace without industry stagnating in their idleness."

9

Only four centuries, he concludes, are worthy of the attention of a philosopher, the age of Philip and Alexander, the age of Cæsar and Augustus, the Italian Renaissance, and finally, the Grand Siècle.[1]

This absolutism of judgement, of course, has its roots in the literary culture of the Renaissance, which revived in an abstract form the old dualism of Hellenism and barbarism and thus for the first time introduced a cleavage between the facts of social development and the ideals of the educated classes.

But by the 18th century this artificial literary ideal had been powerfully reinforced by a no less important philosophical and scientific absolutism that had its origin in the Cartesian movement. The latter was the parent of modern rationalism, not on account of its exaltation of reason, for that had been equally characteristic of the Aristotelian tradition. The originality of Descartes consisted rather in his complete divorce of the human mind as a thinking substance from any dependence on, or even any apparent relation to, the body which it informs and the conditions of physical existence with which it appears to be bound up. The human reason without recourse either to experience or to authority is able to deduce an absolutely certain and complete knowledge from the clear and simple truths which are innate in its own being and which it comprehends by a direct act of intuition.

This is the foundation of the Cartesian method for the reform of the whole body of the sciences. All the vast accumulation of knowledge and tradition which was the heritage of European culture, all the ideas

[1] Voltaire, *Siècle de Louis XIV*, ch. I.

and beliefs that men acquire from experience and literature and the contact with other minds were to be set aside as an impure and uncertain compound of truth and error, and to be replaced by a new knowledge of mathematical certitude which was derived from the infallible light of the pure reason. The simple reasonings of an intelligent man—*un homme de bon sens* —are, he says, of more value than all the learning to be acquired from books and the schools, for they are founded on a direct intuitive certitude that cannot be deceived.

This attitude of mind produced an extraordinary impression on the thought of the age. It was responsible for the formation of those abstract ideas— Reason, Science, Progress, and Civilization, which became the idols of the new age. Fontenelle is the first to speak of " the scientific spirit," and he ascribes its origin to the new temper of thought introduced by Descartes, which was of even greater importance than the philosophy itself.

It is true that the superstructure of Cartesian science was not accepted by the men of the 18th century. On the contrary they ridiculed his deductive system of physics and his ambitious attempt to reconstruct the universe from the simple mathematical laws of extension and movement, and they turned with the enthusiasm of converts to the inductive methods of the English school. But while they paid verbal homage to Bacon and Newton and Locke as the founders of the only true science, they remained Cartesians in their hearts. They showed none of the cautious agnosticism, or rather fideism, of the English thinkers, for they retained intact the faith of Descartes in the

11

human reason as an infallible authority, and they believed that every belief and every historic institution was to be judged by the standard of absolute rational principles.

This unbounded faith in the power of Reason is manifested in all that the philosophers of the 18th century wrote concerning social and political questions. Above all, the conception of social progress, as elaborated by the Abbé St. Pierre, Turgot and Condorcet, was almost exclusively intellectual. Morals were regarded as the static element which had little direct influence on human progress. For example, Helvetius remarks, with all the naïve philistinism of the Enlightenment, that the influence of moral virtue is restricted to the few individuals with whom the sage comes into personal contact, whereas the man who invents a windmill is a benefactor to the whole world.

And if the influence of morals is relatively unimportant, that of religion is positively retrograde. For the men of the Enlightenment viewed Religion— and above all Christianity—as the dark power which is ever clogging and dragging back the human spirit on its path towards progress and happiness. They saw in the development of the historic religions an unrelieved tale of deception and cruelty.

But if the history of the past shows us only the age-long martyrdom of man at the hands of priests and fanatics, the belief in the necessary progress and perfectibility of mankind seems deprived of historical justification, and it is difficult to explain the advance of humanity to perfection and enlightenment in a single bound. In fact the philosophers did not believe in a uniform and gradual process of evolution, but in a sudden advance of the human spirit which had its origin in the philosophic revolution of the Cartesian period. This is the 9th epoch of Condorcet, the century that was marked by the discovery of the true system of the physical universe by Newton, of the science of human nature by Locke and Condillac, and of the science of society by Turgot, Richard Price and Rousseau. This Apocalypse of Reason was preparing the way for a true Millennium—an age when, as Condorcet writes, " the human race, freed from all its fetters, withdrawn from the empire of chance as from that of the enemies of Progress, would walk with firm and assured step in the way of truth, of virtue and of happiness."[1]

These ideas inspired the leaders of the French Revolution in their attempt to refashion society anew. They are clearly expressed in one of the decrees of the Committee of Public Safety in 1794. " The transition of an oppressed nation to democracy," it runs, " is like the effort by which nature rose from nothingness to existence. You must entirely refashion a people whom you wish to make free, destroy its prejudices, alter its habits, limit its necessities, root up its vices, purify its desires."[2]

And the same spirit reappears in the revolutionary political and social reformers of the 19th century, all of whom had an almost apocalyptic belief in the possibility—indeed the certainty—of a complete transformation of human society, an abrupt passage from corruption to perfection, from darkness to light. It is true that the failure of the French Revolution to

---

[1] Condorcet, Œuvres, VI, p. 276.
[2] Cf. Morley, Rousseau, vol. II, p. 132.

realize its promises produced a reaction in the world of thought as well as in the political sphere. But the complete revulsion from the ideas of the 18th century which marked traditionalists like Burke, and de Maistre, and the German Romantic movement, was only temporary. For the most part political and social thinkers remained faithful to the principles of the Enlightenment, they accepted unquestioningly the fundamental ideas of the previous period, above all the conception of Progress, and the idea of an absolute civilization, based on universal principles which were valid for the whole of the human race. They differed from their predecessors only by their distrust of the abstract philosophizing of the 18th century and by their attempt to find a positive and scientific foundation for their theories.

Thus the first half of the 19th century was marked by the first essays towards the constitution of sociology as a true science of society, by the side of, or rather as the crown and completion of, the natural sciences. Even the English Utilitarians, whose minds were still rooted in 18th century habits of thought, show the influence of this new tendency in their efforts to apply a strict scientific method to the problems of population, economic life and legislation, while the Utopian Socialists and anarchists of the Continent, such as Proudhon, went so far as to advocate the supervision of the politician by the scientist, and declared that " the science of government belongs of right to one of the sections of the Academy of Sciences whose permanent secretary is necessarily Prime Minister "[1]

But by far the most important representative of the

[1] *What is Property?* Eng. Tr., p. 265.

14

new scientific tendency in social studies was Auguste Comte, for it was he who first worked out systematically the relation of Sociology to the other sciences. According to his teaching, there is a regular evolution from the abstract and general to the more concrete and particular sciences—from Mathematics to Astronomy and Physics, and so to Chemistry, Biology and Sociology. The development of Sociology marks the final stage of scientific progress, and renders it possible to unite the whole body of knowledge in an organic synthesis. This concrete and positive science of man, and of external nature in relation to man, would automatically supersede all the theological and metaphysical systems which had reigned while the scientific synthesis was still incomplete—they were creatures respectively of the dark and the twilight which disappeared in the light of dawn. Consequently Comte condemned in the strongest terms the whole trend of the 18th century social philosophy and the work of the revolutionary reformers as vitiated by metaphysical presuppositions, and as negative and destructive rather than positive and constructive in its results. Nevertheless this did not lead him, as one might have expected, to abandon the abstract ideas of Humanity, Progress and Civilization, and to concentrate his attention in the study of individuals and the particular societies. On the contrary, he held that the only reality was Humanity, and that the individual man was a pure abstraction— that all the observable changes of particular societies were conditioned by the Law of Progress, which was the ultimate fact of positive social science.

Moreover, since the scientific synthesis which was the result of the positive philosophy was essentially sociological, it followed that nature was to be interpreted in terms of society, and not regarded as the greater whole of which society forms a dependent part. In the eyes of Comte, the function of science was strictly limited to the service of humanity, and he condemns the pursuit of knowledge for its own sake, as, for example, in the case of astronomy outside the solar system, or pure mathematics which bear no practical fruit in physics or mechanics, no less strongly than the speculations of the metaphysician and the theologian.

It is true that Comte fully admitted the relativity of the resultant positive synthesis. But since he rejected the possibility of an absolute synthesis, of any interpretation of reality in terms of the whole, the dualism between human values and external nature could only be solved by the complete subordination of scientific and philosophic activity to human ends. Thus Comte's denial of all metaphysical or theological conceptions, instead of leading to materialism, finally ended in a religious system in which the temporal order would be subordinated to the Spiritual Power represented by the priests of Humanity and Progress, and both science and action would be consecrated to the service and worship of a quasi-transcendent Great Being. It is not surprising that this solution failed to satisfy the 19th century world. The philosopher who, in his later years, systematically refused to study not only newspapers, but even all scientific and philosophical publications, and read practically nothing besides his Dante and his Thomas à Kempis was not likely to be accepted as a pontiff by the party of " progress and enlightenment." His traditionalism

and his religiosity were thoroughly distasteful to the
liberal and the rationalists, while the severe limitations that he imposed on scientific method were equally
inacceptable to the buoyant optimism of 19th century
science, then in the full tide of its triumphant advance.

By 1848 the influence of the romantic idealism
which had dominated European thought during the
early part of the century was on the ebb, and the
current was once more setting strongly in the direction
of materialism. Even in Germany, the home of
idealist philosophy, scientific materialism was now
dominant, and found expression in the most naïve
and exaggerated forms, for example, in Buchner's comparison of the relation between body and mind to
that of a steam engine and the power it generates.
Above all the progress of biological studies and the
rise of the doctrine of evolution had a powerful influence
on social thought. This is especially characteristic of
the work of Herbert Spencer, perhaps the most representative sociologist of the 19th century. The doctrine
of Evolution is the key-note of his whole philosophy.
He regards social progress as one instance of a universal
cosmic law. It is not merely analogous to, but identical
with, the law of physical and biological evolution.
In the words of a writer of the period : " The progress
of Civilization figures merely as one illustration more
of a law that has necessitated alike the formation of
solar systems from misty nebulæ; of mountain and
river and meadow from the original murky incan-
descent ball of earth ; and of the bright and infinite
variety of animal and vegetable forms from a few
primitive simple germs : the great Law of Evolution
whereby all things that exist must pass from the simple

17

to the multiform, from the incoherent to the coherent, from the indefinite to the definite; the law which, while determining not only that the egg with its simple uniform composition shall gradually unfold itself into the chick with its complex coherent and definite system of functions and organs; that the worm ' striving to be man, shall mount through all the spires of form ' ; determines also that Human society itself, which starts from the condition in which each family wanders about alone and isolated, and each man is at once warrior, hunter, fisherman, tool-maker and builder, shall pass through the nomadic stage in which several families are united in a kind of chieftainship, where the king is at once priest and judge, and the priest at once judge and king, and eventuate in those complex settled states of Modern Civilization where labour is carried to its minutest subdivision and every function finds its appropriate social organ."[1]

Here we have the idea of Progress arrived at its full expansion, and embracing not only the life of man, but the whole order of nature. It remained, however, a philosophic rather than a scientific theory, for Spencer had already developed his general theory of evolution before he applied it to biology, and even his biological views were reached independently of Darwin, whose " Origin of Species " appeared two years later than Spencer's essay on " Progress: its Law and Cause," at the time when the latter had already planned his Synthetic Philosophy. Nevertheless there was a contradiction between the 18th century ideal of Progress and the new scientific interpretation

[1] J. B. Crozier, *Civilization and Progress: Being the Outlines of a New System of Political, Religious and Social Philosophy* (London, 1885), p. 385.

18

of it. The 18th century philosophers, even when they were materialists, placed man in a category above and apart from the rest of nature, and hypostatized human reason into a principle of world development. But the new evolutionary theory put man back into nature, and ascribed his development to the mechanical operation of the same blind forces which ruled the material world. Thus Reason becomes merely an organ that has been developed by man's effort to adapt himself to his environment, and is as essentially related to his struggle for existence as is the speed of the deer or the scent of the beast of prey.

It is true that the earliest form of the evolutionary theory as set forth by Lamarck, who was a Deist and a disciple of Condorcet, was still dominated by this optimistic and teleological doctrine of Progress. But the new scientific method eliminated all such teleological conceptions. The biology of Darwin and also the biological philosophy of Spencer had arisen under the influence of the objective and pessimistic views of Malthus. The theory of Natural Selection —the Survival of the Fittest, to use Spencer's famous phrase—was the Malthusian law of the pressure of population upon food supply elevated into a biological principle. It was a law of Progress, but blind non-ethical progress, in which suffering and death played a larger part than foresight or co-operation. "From the war of nature," writes Darwin, "from famine and death, the most exalted object that we are capable of conceiving, namely the production of the higher animals, directly results."

The application of this doctrine to social life would seem to subvert the humanitarian ideals of fraternity

19

and social benevolence which had been characteristic of the older doctrine of progress, and to lead inevitably to the cult of individual egotism and social militarism. It is true that Spencer, in spite of his acceptance of the Survival of the Fittest as a social principle and his resultant opposition to state intervention in such matters as poor relief and social legislation, did not draw these extreme conclusions. On the one hand, he was able to counterbalance the factor of natural selection by the Lamarckian principle of the inheritance of acquired characteristics, and on the other, his instinctive hatred of militarism led him to elaborate a peculiar and somewhat inconsistent theory, according to which the system of political centralization and military organization which corresponds to the brain and the nervous system in the individual organism must give place to industrialism which is the social counterpart of the nutritive system, so that the process of social development would seem to lead to the increasing predominance of the stomach over the brain.

But those who, unlike Spencer, accepted wholeheartedly the Darwinian theory of Natural Selection had to face the consequences of this profound contradiction between their scientific beliefs and their ethical ideals. In place of the optimism of the 18th century thinkers who saw Nature as

" The World's great Harmony, that springs
From Union, Order, full Consent of things."

so that " the state of Nature was the Reign of God," they had to admit that man, for all his high hopes and spiritual idealism, was the product and plaything of a "Nature red in tooth and claw," which would eventually devour its own offspring. This contradiction was fully realized by some of the most popular exponents of the new scientific world view. Huxley, above all, is never tired of insisting in the non-moral character of the evolutionary process, and he even defended the pessimism of Calvinistic theology as more in harmony with scientific truth than the popular optimism which regarded human nature as good and the cosmic process as necessarily progressive. " Social Progress," he writes, " means the checking of the cosmic process at every step, and the substitution for it of another, which may be called ethical progress."

But if this is so, we cannot hope that man's puny efforts will avail against the eternal course of nature. We are led inevitably to the defiant pessimism which Mr. Bertrand Russell has expressed so eloquently in " A Freeman's Worship ": " Brief and powerless is man's life ; on him and all his race the slow sure doom falls pitiless and dark. Blind to good and evil, reckless of destruction, omnipotent matter rolls on its relentless way ; for man, condemned to-day to lose his dearest, to-morrow himself to pass through the gates of darkness, it remains only to cherish ere yet the blow falls, the lofty thoughts that ennoble his little day ; disclaiming the coward terrors of the slave of Fate, to worship at the shrine that his own hands have built ; undismayed by the empire of chance, to preserve a mind free from the wanton tyranny that rules his outward life ; proudly defiant of the irresistible forces that tolerate for a moment his knowledge and his condemnation, to sustain alone a weary but unyielding Atlas, the world that his own ideals have fashioned despite the trampling march of unconscious power."[1]

But this Promethean altitude can never be adopted by the ordinary man. Unless men believe that they have an all-powerful ally outside time, they will inevitably abandon the ideal of a supernatural or anti-natural moral progress, and make the best of the world as they find it, conforming themselves to the law of self-interest and self-preservation which governs the rest of nature. And thus the philosophy of Progress, which had inspired such boundless hopes for the future of the human race, resulted in negation and disillusionment. The Cartesian Reason, which had entered so triumphantly on its career of explaining nature and man to itself by its own unaided power, ended in a kind of rational suicide by explaining itself away.

Hence it is easy to understand the causes of the anti-rational and anti-intellectualist reaction, which set in at the close of the 19th century. In every field of thought there was a tendency to dethrone the intellect from its former position of undisputed supremacy. In philosophy we have Pragmatism and Vitalism, and in psychology the anti-intellectualist theories of the Psychoanalysts and the Behaviourists. In sociology the same tendency shows itself in the new emphasis laid on the non-rational side of social life, as manifested in crowd psychology and " herd instinct," and still more in the vitalist social theory of George Sorel, the philosopher of Syndicalism. Nevertheless, the absolute ideas that had governed social thought since the 18th century had entered too deeply into the mind of the

[1] *Mysticism and Logic*, p. 56.

22

average man to be easily shaken off. Even when he had lost his faith in Reason, he still believed in science, and in the final character of the new scientific culture. He believed as firmly as ever that the particular and local civilization of Western Europe was Civilization in the absolute sense, and that it was the necessary culmination of a continuous unilinear movement of progress, which led from savagery upwards through the ancient oriental and classical civilizations to the modern industrial-scientific order. The criticism of these conceptions did not come from the sociologists. As the rationalists had destroyed men's faith in Reason, so it was the work of the historians to undermine men's belief in the unity of History.

II

HISTORY AND THE IDEA OF PROGRESS

THE movement of scientific rationalism which was described in the last chapter does not represent the whole development of European thought in the 19th century. In fact, that age was more lacking in intellectual and spiritual unity than any period of history since the Renaissance. If the 19th century was the age of science and rationalism, it was no less the age of romanticism and imagination. Above all, it was the age of History, when for the first time men set themselves to re-create the past, and sought to enter with imaginative sympathy into the life and thought of past ages and of different peoples.

It is owing to this historical sense that the modern Western European differs most profoundly from the men of other ages and cultures. World history means infinitely more to him than it meant to the ancient Greek or Oriental thinkers. To the latter, Time, and consequently History, were without ultimate value or significance; to the modern European they are the very foundation of his conception of reality. Yet this sense of history found no adequate expression in the movement of scientific rationalism. The philosophers and scientists of the 18th and 19th centuries viewed the universe from the point of view of the physicist, as a mechanical system, a closed order ruled by mathematical law, rather than as the manifestation of living spirit. And the 18th century historians were equally limited in their outlook. They concentrate their attention on facts and events; they accumulate masses of detail, without giving any heed to the informing spirit, which alone can give significance to the material circumstances. They view History as a sequence of detached events, instead of a life process.

The new current of thought which had so great an influence on 19th century culture had its origins in Germany, just as the movement of scientific enlightenment had its birth in France. For centuries the cultural life of central Europe had been dependent upon the more advanced civilization of the West, and it was not until the close of the 18th century that Germany once more began to play an independent part in the international life of Europe. But the last quarter of the 18th century and the first quarter of the 19th witnessed a great intellectual awakening. It was the age of classical German literature, of Schiller and Goethe, and of the new Romantic movement, which had its centre in Berlin, the classical age of music which attained its climax in the work of Mozart and Beethoven, above all it was the classical age of German philosophy—the age of Kant and Fichte, of Schelling and Schleiermacher and Hegel.

Although this new German culture had arisen under the influence of the French thought of the age of Enlightenment, its spirit was utterly different from that of the French philosophic rationalism, and still

25

more from the practical and utilitarian thought of contemporary England. It revolted alike from the mechanical and mathematical conception of nature, and from the individualist and utilitarian idea of society. In contrast to the brilliant and superficial rationalism of French thought with its cult of " les idées claires," its ideal of knowledge was not rational analysis, but that direct intuition of reality by imaginative vision which unites the mind with its object in a kind of vital communion. This transfusion of thought and reality found its extreme development in the Romantic writers, above all in Novalis' mystical sense of union with Nature, but it is hardly less characteristic of Goethe, classicist though he was. " My thought," he says, " is inseparable from its objects—my intuition is itself a thought, and my thought an intuition." And again in Faust, " Dost thou not feel in thy heart the action of an unknown power which hovers about thee, visible in an invisible mystery? Fill thy soul with it, and when thou hast found happiness in this feeling, call it what thou wilt; call it Joy, Heart, Love, God, I have no name for it. All is feeling."

The same ideal dominates the German philosophy. It is true that the claims of Reason have never been put more strongly than by Fichte and Schelling and Hegel. But there is a world of difference between their Reason and that of the rationalists. It is in fact not the discursive analytic reason, but the higher reason, the " Intellectus " of the schoolmen, which is independent of sensible experience and is capable of comprehending pure and absolute being in an act of simple intuition. It is a law to itself, the creative power which lies behind the phenomenal world and from which the latter derives its reality.

This conception of knowledge stands in complete contrast to the methods of modern physical science, which tend to identify the ultimate reality of nature with those quantitive relations that are susceptible of mathematical treatment and treat the so-called " secondary qualities," such as colour and sound, as purely subjective and unreal.

Accordingly we find the German thinkers of the early 19th century in revolt against the whole Newtonian tradition. Goethe himself attempted to replace Newton's theory of optics by a new " Farbenlehre," based on the essentially qualitative distinction of colours, while Hegel carried the reaction against Newton to its extreme limits,[1] and constructed a " Philosophy of Nature " which is more widely removed from modern scientific thought than are the systems of Plato and Aristotle. German philosophical thought abolished the opposition between matter and spirit—the dualism of the external and the inner worlds. Fichte writes : " In all the forms that surround me I behold the reflection of my own being, broken up into countless diversified shapes." " The dead heavy mass, which only filled up space, has vanished ; and in its place there flows onward, with the rushing movement of mighty waves, an eternal stream of life and power and action which issues forth from the original source of all life."[2] The German view of life is in fact musical rather than mathematical. The

---

[1] " Three times," he says, " has an apple proved fatal. First to the human race in the fall of Adam, secondly to Troy through the gift of Paris, and last of all to science through the fall of Newton's apple."—*Werke* XVI, 17.

[2] Fichte, *The Vocation of Man*, tr. W. Smith, p. 172. (Ed. Ritchie, 1906.)

27

unity of existence is a kind of vital rhythm which reconciles opposite and apparently irreconcilable realities into an ultimate harmony. In the words of Goethe's Earth Spirit, it is

"Geburt und Grab
Ein wechselnd Weben
Ein glühend Leben
So schaf' ich am sausenden Webstühl der Zeit
Und wirke der Gottheit lebendiges Kleid." [1]

Hence an entirely new attitude to history and society. A people is not an accumulation of separate individuals artificially united by conscious agreement for their mutual advantage, as Locke and the French philosophers had taught; it is a spiritual unity for which and by which its members exist.

This conception first found expression in the writings of Herder, who used the idea of a " collective soul " to explain the development of literature and art. For him civilization is not the abstract unity of the French philosophers, it is " an individual good that is everywhere climatic and organic, the offspring of tradition and custom." He regarded poetry as " a kind of Proteus among the peoples, which changes its form according to language, manners, habits, according to temperament and climate, nay even according to the accent of different nations." This concentration upon the diversity of historical and national genius, as opposed to the uniformity of the classical tradition was to be the distinguishing feature

---

[1] " Birth and Death, a changing web, a glowing Life. Thus do I work at the humming loom of Time and fashion the living garment of God."

of the Romantic movement of which Herder was the chief pioneer. For in that movement the peoples of Northern and Western Europe, above all the Germans, rediscovered their own mediæval past with something of the same enthusiasm and wonder which Renaissance Italy experienced at the recovery of classical antiquity. For the first time since the 16th century the art and culture of the Middle Ages was realized and appreciated. To the men of the early 19th century, it was like the discovery of a new world, and it provoked a general reaction against the whole rationalist culture of the previous age.

In political thought this romantic conception of the " collective soul " of a people found full expression in Fichte's famous Addresses to the German People in 1807 which became the foundation of a theory of Nationalism and of the rights of the national spirit which was to dominate 19th century thought. And the same idea inspired Hegel's philosophy of the State and of History. To Hegel the state is the supreme reality which possesses a plentitude and self-sufficiency of being far surpassing that of the individual. It is nothing less than " the Incarnation of the Divine Idea as it exists on Earth." It manifests itself not merely in politics, but in religion, in philosophy and in art, all of which are the expressions of the Spirit of the people or the age. " These various forms are inseparably united with the spirit of the State. Only in connection with this particular religion can this particular political constitution exist; just as in such and such a state, such and such a Philosophy, or order of Art."[1] Hence Hegel regards History

[1] *Philosophy of History.* Tr. J. Sibree. London 1857, p. 55.

as the highest form of knowledge. Physical science can only show us the eternal cyclic repetition of phenomenal change, while universal History is the progressive manifestation and self-realization of the absolute spirit in Time. Thus the reality and value of the external world, which idealism had tended to deny in respect to Nature, is restored and given a transcendent significance. For in History the Real is the Ideal, " the rational necessary course of the World Spirit, and that spirit whose nature is always one and the same, but which unfolds this its one nature in the phenomena of the world's existence."

This exalted conception of the function of History had a great effect in 19th century thought. It influenced the rise of the German historical school which began with Niebuhr and Savigny and reached its full development in the work of Ranke and Mommsen. Unfortunately Hegel's deification of the State, and in particular of the Prussian State—had a disastrous effect on the later developments. The thought of both Fichte and Hegel was affected by their realization of Germany's need for national unification, and this caused them to idealize the national state rather than the common culture to which Germany actually owed such unity as she possessed. The professional historians did nothing to restore the balance, for both in Germany and in this country state-worship and a strong nationalistic bias continued to characterize the writing of history. Treitschke and Froude are only the extreme examples of this tendency. Consequently political and constitutional history did not lead up to the general study of cultures or of civilization as a whole which had been the Hegelian ideal. The only general discipline was a so-called "Science of Politics" which meant little more than the history of political ideas. Moreover the 19th century historians were diverted from a study of the wider aspects of cultural history by the immense and necessary labour of documentary research and the criticism of sources, and it was not until the close of the century that historians, at least such German historians as Karl Lamprecht and Eduard Meyer, began once more to take up the work of historical synthesis which had been in abeyance for two generations.

Nevertheless the State still remained the centre of interest to the historians, and it was only in the more specialized branches of knowledge, such as archæology, ethnology, and the history of art and literature, that the cultural rather than the political unity was taken as the object of study. The general transference of interest from political history to the comparative study of cultures did not take place until the close of the Great War and the downfall of the political system in which Germany had set her faith for a century. Even then the work which, more than any other, marked the change of opinion was due not to a professional historian but to a journalist. The enormous success of Herr Spengler's *Decline of the West* [1] was indeed principally due to the way in which its thesis appealed to the pessimism and disillusionment of the defeated peoples. Nevertheless it was also the logical, if extreme, conclusion of a current of thought which reached back to the Romantic epoch. Although it is dominated by a spirit of

[1] O. Spengler, *Der Untergang des Abendlandes*, 2 vols, 1920-1922. Eng. trans., 1926-1928.

relativism and anti-intellectualism, in contradiction to the optimist absolutism of the earlier philosophy, its points of contact with the Romantic view of history and the Hegelian social philosophy are numerous and evident enough.

To Spengler, as to Hegel, World History is nothing less than a " second Cosmos " with a different content and a different law of movement from that of the " First Cosmos "—Nature—which has hitherto absorbed the attention of the scientist. It has its own internal law—Schicksal or Destiny, as distinguished from the law of Causality, which rules the world of Nature. That is to say, historical time is not mere numerical succession, it is the registration of a life process like the years of a man's life. Until the unities that lie behind the time-cycles of history have been grasped, it is useless to try to explain historical change by secondary causes. But if it is possible to attain an internal knowledge of history, if we could grasp intuitively the principle that gives unity to an age or to a culture, then history will take an organic form, and we shall be able to see in all historic phenomena the expression of a moulding force behind the play of circumstances.

This unifying principle Herr Spengler finds in the spirit of the great world-cultures. He claims that each culture has an individual style or personality, which can be seized intuitively by whoever possesses a feeling for history, just as the individual genius of a great musician or artist can be recognized by the born critic in all his works. This individual style is not confined to the art or the social forms of a culture, as some have thought; it extends to philosophic thought, to science and to mathematics. Each culture has its distinctive *number*, so that there is a deep inner bond between the geometry of Euclid and the Greek tragedy, between algebra and arabesque, between the differential calculus and contrapuntal music. This principle of the organic interconnection of all the expressions of a particular culture is carried by Herr Spengler to paradoxical lengths. He maintains that there is an "intimate dependence of the most modern physical and chemical theories on the mythological conceptions of our Germanic forefathers"; that Perspective in Painting, Printing, Credit, Long Range Artillery and Contrapuntal Music, are all of them expressions of one psychic principle, while the City State, the nude statue, Euclid and the Greek coin are alike expressions of another.[1] There is, in fact, no human activity which is not the vehicle of the cultural soul; the most abstract scientific thought and the most absolute ethical systems are partial manifestations of a process which is bound up with a particular people and a geographical region, and have no validity outside the domain of their own culture.

This leads to the most fundamental philosophic relativism. "There are no eternal truths. Each philosophy is an expression of its own age, and only of its own age, and there are no two ages which possess the same philosophical intentions."[2] The vital question for a philosopher is whether he embodies the *Zeitgeist*, "whether it is the soul of the age itself which speaks by his works and intuitions." Hitherto the philosophers have had no inkling of this truth. They have exalted the standards of conduct and

[1] Op. cit. I, p. 66.   [2] Op. cit. I, p. 58.

33

the laws of thought of the modern Western European into absolute laws for humanity, they have not realized the possibility of a different soul and a different truth from their own. The historians have shared their error. The civilization that they saw around them was " Civilization," the movement that brought it to maturity was " Progress." They did not dream that European civilization was a limited episode like the civilizations of China and Yucatan.

The time has come, Herr Spengler says, to make a revolution comparable to the abandonment of the geocentric astronomy, to introduce a new " Copernican " philosophy of history, which will study each culture by the laws of its own development, which will not subordinate the past to the present, or interpret the souls of other cultures by the standards that are peculiar to our own. The task of the true historian then must be to write the biographies of the great cultures as self-contained wholes, which follow a similar course of growth and decay, but are as unrelated to one another as different planetary systems. These great cultures are eight in number, Egypt, Babylonia, India, China, the Maya culture of Central America, the culture of Classical Antiquity, the Arabian culture and the culture of Western Europe. There are, in addition, a few cultures which have failed to attain full development, such as those of the Hittites, the Persians and the Quichua.

The spring-time of a new culture is seen in the rise of a new mythology, which finds expression in the heroic saga and epic. Herr Spengler instances the Vedic mythology for India, the Olympian mythology and the Homeric poems for Antiquity, primitive Christianity

34

and the Gospels for the "Arabian" culture, and "Germanic Catholicism" and the Nibelungenlied for Western Europe. In the next stage—"Summer"— the culture attains to full self-consciousness. This is the time of the rise of the characteristic philosophies, and the building up of a new mathematic, which is, in Herr Spengler's view, perhaps the most fundamental criterion by which to fathom the essence of a culture. Pythagoras and Descartes, Parmenides and Galileo are the representatives of this phase.

"Autumn" is marked by a loosening of social co-hesion, by the growth of rationalism and individualism. At the same time, the creative power of a culture finds its final expression in the great conclusive philo-sophical systems, and in the work of the great mathe-maticians. It is the period of Plato and Aristotle, of Goethe and Kant, but also of the Sophists and the Encyclopædists.

In "Winter" the inner development of a culture is complete. After the triumph of the irreligious and materialistic *Weltanschauung*, "Culture" passes away into "Civilization," which is its inorganic, fossilized counterpart, and which finds its spiritual expression in a cosmopolitan and ethical propaganda, such as Buddhism, Stoicism and 19th century Social-ism. A similar course of development is traced in art, in economics and in political organizations; and at the root of the whole process lies the physical unity of a people or a race, so that the passing of a Culture into a Civilization is at the same time the decomposition of an ethnic organism from its living state into the formlessness of cosmopolitanism and race mixture, which produces a new mongrel population of "déracinés."

Every historic culture must pass through this life process, just as every human being must pass through the same life-cycle from birth to death. And consequently each phase in the life of a particular culture finds its analogy in every other culture. Each event or personality possesses not only a local and temporary importance, it has also a symbolic meaning, as the temporary representative of a universal type. There is not merely a superficial historical parallel, there is an organic identity between the place of Napoleon in our culture and that of Alexander in antiquity, between the Sophists and the Encyclopædists, between the Ramessides and the Antonines. This principle is of the greatest importance for Herr Spengler's theory. By its use he claims that it will be possible not only to reconstruct vanished civilizations, as the palæontologist reconstructs some prehistoric creature from a single bone, but even to establish a law for the " Predetermination of History," so that, when once the underlying idea of a culture has been grasped, it will be possible to foretell the whole course of its growth and the actual dates of its principal phases.

Herr Spengler's aim throughout his work is in fact a practical one. He wishes to plot out the descending curve of Western Civilization, to make the present generation conscious of the crisis through which it is passing and of the true task that lies before it. *Der Untergang des Abendlandes* is nothing else but the final passing of the Western Culture and the coming of " Civilization." Consequently, the " architectonic " possibilities of the Western soul have been realized, and there remains only the practical task of conservation. The age has no more a need of artists and philosophers and poets, it calls for men of " Roman hardness," engineers, financiers, and organizers, of the type of Cecil Rhodes.

It is Herr Spengler's desire that the men of the new generation should turn to " der Technik statt der Lyrik, der Marine statt der Malerei, der Politik statt der Erkentnisskritik."[1] The governing movement of the new age is to be Socialism, not the Socialism of the idealist or the revolutionary, but a practical, organizing, imperialist Socialism which stands as far from the latter, as did the world city of the Roman lawyer and governor from the world City of the Stoic theorists.

The culture of the West stands to-day where the ancient world stood in the age of the Roman conquest, when Rome was taking the place of the Hellenistic states. The empty forms of Democracy and con-stitutionalism must pass away before the coming of a new Cæsarism which will subordinate both the selfishness of class interests and the idealism of social reformers to the practical task of world organization. " Die Träume der Weltverbesserer sind Werkzeuge von Herrennaturen geworden."[2]

To the English mind, ever suspicious of the theorist and perhaps of the historical theorist more than all others, these views may seem so fantastic as to be hardly worthy of consideration. But this is largely due to a difference of historical outlook. Even in this cosmopolitan age the different European peoples have each preserved their own separate views of the past,

[1] Op. cit. I, p. 57: " The technical instead of the lyrical; shipping instead of painting; politics instead of epistemology."
[2] " The dreams of the world reformers have become the tools of the men of action."

and the man who has been brought up on the tradition of Macaulay and Freeman and Grote and Stubbs will never understand his contemporary who lives under the tradition of Treitschke and Mommsen. This opposition is sometimes softened by the existence of a liberal current of opinion in Germany which has been affected by the thought of the Western peoples, but Herr Spengler is a pure Central European, who views the whole history of Europe from the longitude of Munich and Berlin. The Baroque monarchies, which to the ordinary Englishman are a byeway of history, are to him the characteristic expression of Western culture at the moment when it had achieved its final form, while Parliamentarism and democracy, which to us are central, are to him the phenomena of decline. This difference of outlook makes his book all the more interesting for a foreigner, but it has the disadvantage of distracting the reader's attention from Herr Spengler's essential thesis to those details of his historical interpretation which arouse instinctive prejudice. If we disregard these accidental peculiarities, we shall see that *The Decline of the West* is only an extreme statement of the new relativist attitude to history which has become almost universal. During the last ten or twenty years there has been a general reaction against the old absolutist view of civilization and against that unquestioning faith in the transcendent value of our own Western culture which marked the 19th century. There are civilizations, but no *Civilization ;* and the standards and achievements of each culture are valid only within the limits of that culture ; they possess no absolute significance.

38

It is obvious that this philosophy of history can find no room for the conception of Progress. There is certainly a process of evolution, but it is a blind movement, which has no ethical meaning, such as was essential to the old idea of Progress. For Herr Spengler each culture is a fixed organism, which ends in itself, and it is no more possible to believe that the Hellenic culture and that of modern Europe are successive steps on the part of the Progress of Humanity, than it would be to suppose that the pug and the Pomeranian are necessary stages in the upward progress of Doghood to perfection.

Hence the development of culture is not merely non-ethical; it is irrational. History is essentially unintelligible: for the law of Destiny, not that of Causality, is the law of life. The makers of history, the men and peoples of Destiny are unconscious and instinctive in their creative activity, while the thinkers —philosophers and men of science—are sterile systematizers, " bloodless " men who have lost touch with the vital forces of their culture. Consequently, Spengler is continually depreciating Reason and scientific analysis, in comparison with instinctive feeling or " the physiognomic tact " which is the only means of approach to the positive aspect of reality which he so characteristically terms " the totemistic side of life." For him the roots of historical change—that is to say of historical reality lie not in the Reason but in " the blood."

If this is true, it is clear that culture is exclusively the result of racial growth, and owes nothing to Reason or to any tradition which transcends the limits of a single people's experience. For each culture is a world to itself, hermetically sealed against every influence from without, and impenetrable to the eyes of the rest of the world. And Herr Spengler fails to explain how he or anyone else can grasp the life process of a different organism from that of which he forms part even by the exercise of " physiognomic tact." But this idea is irreconcilable with the whole course of human history, which is nothing but a vast system of intercultural relations.

Even in external things, we see how the life of a people can be transformed by some invention or art of life that has been borrowed from without, as in the case of the introduction of the horse among the American Indians by the Spaniards.

Far more important, however, is the spread of new forms of thought. It is true that a philosopher like Aristotle, or a religious leader like Mohammed, is the offspring of a particular culture, and could not have appeared in any other land, or at any other period but his own. Nevertheless, the influence of such men far transcends cultural and racial boundaries. It is true that by becoming a Moslem the negro or the Turk undergoes a cultural transformation; a new cultural type arises which is neither that of Moslem Arabia nor that of the native pagan people. But the fact that such a process can occur at all is fatal to the Spenglerian theory of absolutely isolated and unrelated culture cycles. It readmits the principle of causality and the opportunity for rational analysis which Spengler professes to banish for ever. And even if he denies that such an admixture is a true culture, and relegates the peoples in question to his category of " Fellachen-völker "—" Fellahin peoples,"—can he exclude the factor of alien intellectual influences from the very parent culture itself?

Thus, for example, in dealing with Islam we must not only take account of the culture of the Arabs of Arabia, who created the original Islamic state. There is also the Byzantine Syro-Egyptian culture of the Levant, an old mature civilization which influenced Islam from the cradle; there is the Sassanian-Persian culture, which had a vital influence on Islam even before the days of the Abbasids; there is the culture of Khorasan and Trans-Oxiana, mainly Persian, but possibly containing a Bactrian Greek element, and certainly affected by Indian Buddhist influence; finally there are the non-cultured peoples—the Turks, who were for centuries in contact with Persian and Chinese civilization, the Berbers, who had previously been under the influence of the Roman-Hellenistic culture, and last of all the negroes. All these cultures and peoples brought their contributions to the civilization of mediæval Islam, so that under the surface uniformity of Arabic language and religion and institutions, an extraordinary process of fermentation and change was taking place.

Hence it is clear that, in order to explain the life of civilizations, it is not sufficient to possess a formula for the life-cycle of individual peoples, we must also understand the laws of cultural interaction and the causes of the rise and fall of the great cultural syncretisms, which seem to overshadow the destinies of individual peoples. Considered from this point of view, the last stage of a culture, the phase to which Herr Spengler confines the name of " Civilizations," acquires peculiar importance. It is not merely a negative period of petrifaction and death, as he describes it; it is the time when civilization

is most open to external influence. The true significance of the Roman-Hellenistic period, for example, is
not decay, but syncretism. Two different streams of
culture, which we describe loosely as " Oriental " and
" Western," as " Asiatic " and " European," flowed
for several centuries in the same bed, mingling with
one another to such a degree that they seemed to form
a new civilization. And this intermingling of culture
was not merely of importance for the past as the conclusion of the old world, it had a decisive influence on
the future. The passing of an ancient civilization and
the coming of a new age is marked, it is true, by these
two streams once more separating and flowing out
again to East and West as the new daughter cultures
of Islam and Western Europe, though the central river
bed is still occupied for a time by the dwindling stream
of the Byzantine civilization. Nevertheless the two
streams continued to bear witness to their common
origin. The West was moulded by a religion of the
Levant, the East carried on for centuries the tradition
of Hellenic philosophy and science. Aristotle and
Galen travelled to India with the Moslems, to Scotland and Scandinavia with the Christians. Roman
law lived on, alike with the mediæval canonists and the
Ulema of Islam. But because Islam inherited so
largely from the Hellenistic-Oriental culture of Roman
times, Herr Spengler is not justified in giving an Arabic
origin to the latter; the Arabs entered into the cultural inheritance in the East, just as the Germanic
peoples did in the West, as heirs not as originators.

And as East and West, each in its own measure, have
received the inheritance of Hellenic culture, so too
is it with the tradition of Israel. Without that tradition

neither Christendom nor Islam is conceivable; each claims it as its peculiar birthright. It is interwoven with the very texture of the Koran; it lives on in modern Europe; indeed it was nowhere stronger than it has been in the new countries—in Calvinist Scotland, in Lutheran Scandinavia, in Puritan New England. And it was in the same age of syncretism, the period of the Hellenistic-Oriental culture, that the Jewish tradition acquired these new contacts and opportunities for expression. Since then the different culture streams have been flowing away from one another, but they still bear the indelible character set upon them by that decisive period of intercourse and fusion.

All this network of cultural influences is viewed by Herr Spengler as essentially external, unreal, and non-vital. The Christianity of the Middle Ages and that of the Patristic period—" Faustian and Magian Christianity," to use his own expression—are for him two different religions, which possess a common terminology and common usages, but are nevertheless each the original expression of an individual soul. And this is the *reductio ad absurdum* of his whole theory, for it involves the conclusion that the culture of the West would have followed an identical course except for empty forms and names, if it had never become Christian, and had never received the inheritance of the Hellenic and Roman culture traditions. The relativist philosophy of history ends by denying the very existence of relations, and dissolves the unity of history into an unintelligible plurality of isolated and sterile culture processes.

Nevertheless the rejection of Herr Spengler's theory does not justify a denial of the objective reality of cultural unity. Philosophic critics of *The Decline of the West*, such as Mr. R. G. Collingwood,[1] tend to regard history as perpetual becoming, a single universal process of world development. Thus Mr. Collingwood maintains that the conception of a culture is purely subjective, and owes its existence to the observing mind. " The cycle is the historian's field of vision at a given moment." " We fabricate periods of history by fastening upon some, to us, particularly luminous point and trying to study it as it actually came into being. We find our mind caught, as it were, by some striking phenomenon—Greek life in the 5th century or the like; and this becomes the nucleus of a group of historical inquiries asking how it arose and how it passed away; what turned into it and what it turned into."

In so far as a culture exists, it rests on the existence of some dominant idea; and since every idea involves its opposite, one culture necessarily passes into another by the natural evolution of thought. In other words two successive cultures are not independent organisms, they are merely the embodiment of a pair of complementary propositions in the process of Neo-Hegelian dialectic.

This idealistic conception of history is even less satisfactory than Spengler's anti-intellectualist relativism. Like the latter, it makes a complete divorce between History and Science and leaves no room for the contributions of the biologist and the anthropologist. For while Spengler regards a culture as an unconscious physical life-process which can only be grasped by a kind of instinctive sense, Mr. Collingwood eliminates the physical and material aspects altogether, and

[1] In *Antiquity*, I, 3. 1927, Sept.

44

treats cultural development as a purely spiritual movement of ideas.

In reality a culture is neither a purely physical process nor an ideal construction. It is a living whole from its roots in the soil and in the simple instinctive life of the shepherd, the fisherman, and the husbandman, up to its flowering in the highest achievements of the artist and the philosopher; just as the individual combines in the substantial unity of his personality the animal life of nutrition and reproduction with the higher activities of reason and intellect. It is impossible to disregard the importance of a material and non-rational element in history. Every culture rests on a foundation of geographical environment and racial inheritance, which conditions its highest activities. The change of culture is not simply a change of thought, it is above all a change of life. The fall of the Hellenic culture was not due to the passing of the Hellenic idea, it was not, as Mr. Collingwood says, " a process that led to the Magian idea by its own inner logic "; on the contrary, the Hellenic idea never died, it is eternal and imperishable, and the decline of the culture was due to a process of social degeneration—the passing of the Greek people from the land that had fed and nursed it into the melting-pot of urban cosmopolitanism. It is even possible for one culture to kill another, as we see in the case of the destruction of the Peruvian civilization by the Spaniards, and in the countless instances in which primitive cultures have withered away on contact with modern European civilization. Nor is it only the lower cultures that are destroyed in this way. There are also instances of highly developed urban civilizations

45

falling a victim to barbarian invaders, as when the flourishing culture of the Danube provinces was wiped out in the 5th century A.D., or when the cities of Eastern Iran were destroyed by the Mongols. The idealist attempt to see in history only the " glory of the Idea mirroring itself in the History of the World,"[1] fares no better than the optimism of Dr. Panglos, and calls forth in the manner of Hegelian dialectic that opposite and complementary view of Candide, which looks on history as an irrational welter of cruelty and destruction in which brute force and blind chance are the only rulers.

Nevertheless though culture is essentially con-ditioned by material factors, these are not all. A culture receives its form from a rational or spiritual element which transcends the limits of racial and geo-graphical conditions. Religion and science do not die with the culture of which they formed part. They are handed on from people to people, and assist as a creative force in the formation of new cultural organ-isms. There are, in fact, two movements in history; one of which is due, as Herr Spengler shows, to the life process of an individual people in contact with a definite geographical environment, while the other is common to a number of different peoples and results from intellectual and religious interaction and syn-thesis. Any attempt to explain history as the exclusive result of one or other of these factors is doomed to failure. Only by taking account of both these move-ments is it possible to understand the history of human development, and to explain the existence of that real element of continuity and integration in history which alone can justify a belief in human progress.

[1] Hegel, *Philosophy of History*, p. 477.

46

III

ANTHROPOLOGY AND THE THEORY OF PROGRESS: THE MATERIAL FOUNDATIONS OF CULTURE

HITHERTO we have said nothing of the sciences of anthropology and ethnology which have as their special province the study of man's origins and the development of primitive societies. For these sciences are of more recent origin than either sociology or the philosophy of history; indeed they have only recently acquired their autonomy, and even at the present day there is considerable difference of opinion with regard to their legitimate methods and scope.

Anthropology, in particular, owes its origin to the Darwinian movement,[1] and its early representatives, such as Tylor, Lewis Morgan and Bastian were inspired by the ideal of applying the Darwinian theory of Evolution to the history of human development. Consequently, like Herbert Spencer, whose teaching also had an important influence on their thought, they tended to regard all social changes as the result

[1] Professor Marrett writes: " Anthropology is the child of Darwin. Darwinism makes it possible. Reject the Darwinian point of view, and you must reject anthropology also." For " anthropology stands or falls with the working hypothesis derived from Darwinism, of a fundamental kinship and continuity amid change between all the forms of human life."—*Anthropology*, by R. R. Marrett, pp. 8 and 11.

of a single immutable law which followed a similar course in every part of the world and amongst every race and people. This point of view is well summarized by one of the leading American anthropologists of the 19th century, D. G. Brinton, in the following passage :

" These two principles or rather demonstrated truths —the unity of the mind of man, and the substantial uniformity of its action under like conditions—form the broad and secure foundations for Ethnic Psychology. . . . As there are conditions that are universal, such as the structure and functions of the body, its general relations to its surroundings, its needs and powers, these developed everywhere at first the like psychical activities or mental expressions. They constitute what Bastian has happily called the ' elementary ideas ' of our species. In all races, over all continents, they present themselves with a wonderful sameness, which led the older students of man to the fallacious supposition that they must have been borrowed from some common centre."[1]

Hence the numerous and striking resemblances that exist between the cultures of primitive peoples in different parts of the world were ascribed, not to any process of culture-contact or borrowing, but to the innate uniformity of the human mind, which was held to follow everywhere the same line of development. Tylor writes : " The institutions of man are as distinctly stratified as the earth on which he lives. They succeed each other in a series substantially uniform over the globe, independent of what seems the comparatively superficial differences of race and

[1] D. Brinton, *The Basis of Social Relation: A Study in Ethnic Psychology*, 1902, p. 20.

48

language, but shaped by similar human nature acting through successively changed conditions in savage, barbaric and civilized life."[1] For example, since totemism is found in Australia as a characteristic institution of one of the most backward and primitive peoples of the world, it was assumed that every people must have passed through a similar stage, and that totemism everywhere precedes the development of more advanced social institutions, even in cases where no trace of it is to be found in historical times.

Hence the anthropologists believed not merely that it was possible to go behind history, but that their new science supplied a series of general laws which explained the whole course of social evolution. They regarded history as non-scientific—a mere literary exercise or a cataloguing of disconnected events, whereas their own theories stood on the higher plane of exact scientific method. They did not realize that nothing is less scientific than to transfer the methods of one science to another, and that theories of social evolution divorced from history become mere *a priori* dogmatism. Nevertheless their point of view long reigned unchallenged, and even to-day it has not lost its influence: in fact it still inspires many popular works on human evolution and the development of society and culture. It was a historian—the late F. W. Maitland—who first pointed out the fallacies that were involved in the evolutionary method, as applied to social science.[1] He showed that if it is applied to the more advanced phases of cultures, it obviously leads to the most extravagant conclusions.

[1] Tylor, *Journal of Anthrop. Inst.*, XVIII (1889), pp. 245-272—*Nineteenth Cent.*, XL, 1896, pp. 81-96.
[2] F. W. Maitland, *The Body Politic* in *Collected Papers*, III, 285-303.

For even if it were possible, as he denies, to establish a regular and unvarying sequence of culture stages, it would still be necessary to prove by historical evidence that a given people had not proceeded directly from A to Z without passing through the intervening phases. " Our Anglo-Saxon ancestors did not arrive at the alphabet or the Nicene Creed by traversing a long series of ' stages,' they leapt to the one and to the other." And if this occurs so often in historic times, why should it not also be possible in the case of primitive peoples with regard to the diffusion of totemism, or the knowledge of metals?

It was Maitland's belief " that by and by anthropology will have the choice between being history and being nothing," and on the whole the developments of the last twenty-five years have justified his opinion. There has been a general reaction among anthropologists in favour of the historical method, and a return to the belief in the importance of cultural contact and diffusion in the history of social development.

This movement has followed an independent course in several different countries. At Maitland's own university of Cambridge, it was represented by the late Dr. Rivers, whose conversion to the historical method was due, not to theoretical considerations, but to the evidence of his own researches into the social organization and development of the Melanesian peoples. He came to see that a primitive culture was not the result of a simple straightforward process of evolution, as he had been taught to believe, but that it had behind it a long and complex history. In

50

order to understand the culture of a Melanesian tribe, it was necessary to reconstruct their social past, to unravel the tangle of their customs and institutions strand by strand, and to trace each element to its ultimate source. By this process of analysis he proved that the apparent uniformity of the culture veiled a whole series of movements of diffusion and assimilation, and that these outlying regions had received cultural influences from the centres of higher civilization in the past. His disciples, Professor Elliot Smith and Professor Perry, carried this principle still farther, and have attempted to show that practically every element of the higher civilization, wherever it may be found, has originated from a common source, and that this original centre of diffusion is to be found in ancient Egypt.

But already some years before the appearance of Dr. Rivers' work on Melanesia, a vigorous attack on the old evolutionary theory of social development had been launched in Germany and Austria by Professor Graebner and Pater Schmidt. Instead of isolating a single class of social phenomena, as the earlier anthropologists have done, and attempting to obtain an inductive law which would supply a general explanation for all facts of that order in whatever region and people they appeared, Herr Graebner studied each culture as an objective whole, every part of which stood in close relation to the rest. Thus he substituted the conception of a culture-complex—*Kulturkreis*—an interrelated group of social phenomena, in place of the Elementary Ideas of Bastian or the quasi-geological stages of Tylor, as the basis of ethnological study, and attempted to trace the process of social development as resulting from the interrelation and expansion of these primary units.

Although the extreme hostility of Graebner and Schmidt to the principle of evolution, and their denial of the possibility of the independent origin of similar features of culture have met with much criticism, their methods have been generally adopted, and to-day both in ethnology and prehistory the analysis and history of cultural units have taken the place of the old unhistorical methods which attempted to explain all social development in terms of a uniform law of progress. The results of the new methods may be well seen in the writings of the members of the American school of anthropology, such as A. L. Kroeber, C. Wissler, R. H. Lowie and A. Goldenwieser, whose work deserves to be better known in this country than is the case at present. It is the great merit of this school that it fully recognizes the complexity of the problems of cultural development, and resists the tendency to over-simplification which has been the bane alike of the evolutionary and the historical schools, as for example in the case of the Pan-Egyptian theories of the disciples of Dr. Rivers in this country.

For even when we admit the importance of the factors of diffusion and borrowing for the development of culture, the historical method can never cover the whole ground or explain the whole content of culture. It only puts back the problem of origins to an earlier stage and a more limited field.

At the root of all cultural development there still lies the life of a human group in its primary relations to its environment and functions, and the study of these relations remains the first task of the anthropologist or sociologist. The latter, however, were at first too much preoccupied with *a priori* theories of evolution and social progress, to devote themselves to a purely objective study of the facts. For example, writers like MacLennan and Lewis Morgan were not content to show the relations of the family organization of primitive peoples to their economic life and general culture, but used the limited facts at their disposal to build up a vast hypothetical scheme of evolution from primitive promiscuity through group marriage and matriarchy to the patriarchal family, and assumed that social organization went through substantially the same phases of development in every part of the world.

The first thoroughly objective study of human life in relation to its geographical environment and its economic functions was due to a man who knew nothing of anthropology and had little sympathy with earlier sociological theories. F. J. Le Play was a Catholic and a Conservative, at once a man of faith and a man of facts, who loved his Europe and desired to bring it back to the foundations of social prosperity, which he believed to be endangered by the doctrines of revolutionary Liberalism. Nevertheless his method of study was more biological and more in harmony with the spirit of Darwin himself than any of the ambitious evolutionary theories of writers like Herbert Spencer or Lewis Morgan.

His great work, *Les Ouvriers Européens*[1], consists of a detailed study of fifty-seven specimen families in different parts of Europe, from the Urals to the Pennines and the Pyrenees, based on the result of the direct observation

[1] 6 vols., 2nd ed. 1879.

53

of their economic life in its adaptation to nature and the social organization. His attention was especially directed to the primary nature-occupations which are the foundations of all material culture. These fundamental types are six in number; first the hunters and food gatherers, secondly the pastoral peoples, thirdly the fishermen of the sea coasts, fourthly the agriculturalists, fifthly the foresters, and sixthly the miners. Not only does each of these types possess its appropriate geographical environment, so that we have in Europe the Samoyede hunters of the Northern tundras, the Tartar nomads of the Eastern steppes, and the fishermen of the Western sea coast, but each of them is also represented in any typical civilized natural region. As has been shown by Professor Geddes and Mr. Victor Branford, who have done so much to introduce and extend the methods of Le Play in this country, every river valley contains, at least potentially and as it were in section, every type of natural occupation, from the shepherd and the miner in the hills, through the woodmen of the uplands to the lowland farmers and the fishermen of the coast.

Nor is the value of this classification restricted to primitive stages of society, for the higher the civilization, the more complete is the interaction and co-operation of these primary occupational types, while the social qualities that have been formed by them will continue to subsist, even in an urbanized society, the vital forces of which are still largely dependent on this rural foundation. Moreover, Le Play's methods are far from being merely heuristic. As Professor Geddes has pointed out, the three factors which Le Play regards as the primary constituents of social life—Place, Work and Family or People, correspond to the biological formula—Environment, Function and Organism, and thus provide a basis for the correlation of sociological and biological science.

In fact the process of the development of a culture has a considerable analogy to that of a biological species or subspecies. A new biological type arises in response to the requirements of the environment, normally perhaps as the result of the segregation of a *community* in a new or changing environment. (How this occurs, whether by selection, adaptation or spontaneous variation, we need not enquire.) So, too, a culture, reduced to its simplest terms, is simply the way of life of a particular people adapted to a special environment; it is the result of an intimate communion between man and the region in which and from which he lives. If this communion endures without change for a sufficiently long period, it will produce not merely a new way of life, but a new type of man— a race as well as a culture. Thus in the western hemisphere each climatic zone possesses its specific racial type, the Negroids of the tropical forest, the Mediterranean race in the warm temperate zone, the Nordic race in the cooler latitudes, and the Lapps of the Arctic regions.

And each of these races formerly possessed, broadly speaking, its own cultural type, so that we may speak interchangeably of Negroid race and Negroid culture, Nordic race and Nordic culture, Arctic race and Arctic culture.

Such a condition is, of course, only possible where conditions of segregation have endured unchanged for vast ages. In other parts of the world, for example in America, a single racial type is diffused from the tropics to the Arctic circle, with the result that the Indians of the tropical forest do not possess the same physical adaptation to the needs of their environment that marks the African negro.

But although a culture is a very different thing from a race, every culture contains the germs of a potential racial differentiation, a fact which may explain the tendency of modern cultural unities to claim a fictitious racial unity and even to create pseudo-races such as the Anglo-Saxon or the Latin. Such potentialities cannot actualize themselves in modern times owing to the lack of isolation and the rapid change of conditions. The most they can do is to produce a certain cultural or national type which manifests itself in the facial expression and bearing, though not in somatic characteristics. But in prehistoric times conditions were different, and it is possible that the early Palæolithic cultures, which possess so remarkable a uniformity over vast distances both of space and time, are the outcome of different ways of life which also produced a racial differentiation, so that the Mousterian culture, for example, corresponds to the process of adaptation which produced the Neanderthal type of man.

Nevertheless, however primitive a culture may be, and however closely it is moulded by geographical and climatic conditions, it is never a mere passive result of material forces. The human factor is always active and creative. No culture could appear poorer and more retrograde than that of the Bushmen hunters of South Africa; it seems the reduction of human life to its barest essentials. And yet it is no

56

necessary product of exterior circumstance; it is the result of a free and intelligent activity, and it expresses itself in an art and a folk-lore far richer and more original than that of many more advanced peoples. So, too, the Eskimo culture of the Arctic is in a sense absolutely dependent on its environment, and yet at the same time it is one of the most remarkable instances of the triumph of man over nature that the world can show.

We do not regard the dependence of an artist on his material as a sign of weakness and lack of skill. On the contrary, the greater the artist, the more fully does he enter into his material, and the more completely does his work conform itself to the qualities of the medium in which it is embodied. In the same way the conformity of a culture to its natural environment is no sign of barbarism. The more a culture advances, the more fully does it express itself in and through its material conditions, and the more intimate is the co-operation between man and nature. Indeed, in the higher cultures, the factor of regional differentiation often asserts itself more fully than in the lower ones. A hunting culture may be uniform throughout half a continent, while a sedentary agricultural one will develop new regional types according to every variation of climate and vegetation. For though the domestication of animals and plants render man in a sense more independent of nature, it also establishes a new bond of union between them. To every type of agriculture, to every group of cultivated plants, there corresponds a special human culture. The olive, the gift of Athene, was the nurse of the Hellenic culture, as the date palm was the Tree of Life to the people of

Babylonia. The wine and olive of the Mediterranean, the rice and mulberry of China, the coco-nut and taro of the Pacific Islands, the maize and tobacco of Central America, all have their corresponding forms of social organization and property, ideals of well-being, habits of work and types of character, as well as a distinct rhythm of life which depends on the cyclic movement of the farmer's year.

This intimate communion of human culture with the soil in which it is rooted shows itself in every aspect of material civilization—in food and clothing, in weapons and tools, in dwellings and settlements, in roads and methods of communication. In every direction, the natural character of the region determines the modes in which a culture will express itself, and these in turn react upon the character of the culture itself. Nevertheless, while the environment conditions a culture, it does not cause it. There is no automatic law which causes man to realize all the possibilities of his environment. Still less does the geographical factor suffice to explain cultural progress and change. If this alone predominated, each race would possess its own way of life, but it would be as uniform and changeless as the life of an animal species. When once a people had adapted itself to its environment, it would remain as it were in a permanent state of equilibrium; its culture would be a fixed and permanent type which would maintain itself from age to age without any substantial change.

Actually there does exist a tendency towards the fixation of culture in permanent unchanging types, whenever a people is left isolated in its natural environment. The time factor is unimportant, for time of itself is not an agent of change. The culture of the South African Bushmen, which we have already mentioned, shows striking points of resemblance to that of the Capsian people of Spain and North Africa in later palæolithic times. In fact there are grounds for supposing that it is actually the same culture and the same race which have maintained themselves intact in the far South, though they have been driven out of their old haunts by the coming of more advanced peoples. So, too, it is possible that the Arctic peoples have preserved the traces of a cultural tradition which goes back to the palæolithic hunters who ranged the steppes of Northern Europe during the later Glacial period.

The fact that this unbroken continuity of cultural type is exceptional, and does not characterize all the so-called primitive peoples, is due, above all, to the rarity of complete isolation. Apart from a few remote or inhospitable areas, such as the steppes of South Africa and Australia, the Arctic regions and the farthest depths of the tropical forest, every part of the world has witnessed an age-long process of contact and intermixture of peoples and cultures. It was the realization of the importance of this factor, in the course of his researches into the history of Melanesian culture, that caused the late Dr. Rivers to revise his whole conception of the causes of social evolution and change. " I was led," he writes, " to the view that the current conception of independent evolution, which I had accepted so blindly, was a fiction. The evidence from Melanesia suggests that an isolated people does not change or advance, but that the introduction of new ideas, new instruments and new techniques leads to a definite process of evolution, the products of which may differ greatly from either the indigenous or the immigrant constituents, the result of the inter-action thus resembling a chemical compound rather than a physical mixture. The study of Melanesian culture suggests that when this newly-set-up process of evolution has reached a certain pitch it comes to an end, and is followed by a period of stagnation which endures until some fresh incoming of external influences sets up a new period of progress."[1]

This limited process of social evolution is the true explanation of that cyclical character of the life of cultures which is the foundation of Herr Spengler's philosophy. The cycle of assimilation and change which goes to produce a new culture occupies a definite limited period, and it is possible that the remarkable similarity in the duration of culture cycles, which has impressed so many thinkers both in the present and the past, may be due to the fact that the process of racial fusion requires a certain number of generations in which to work itself out. For in the majority of cases, the birth of a new culture is due not merely to new influences, but to the coming of a new people, and consequently the change involves a complex process of racial and social readaptation and assimila-tion. We must take account, first, of the action of the new environment on the type of man and society that has grown up in another region, secondly, of the actions and reactions of the cultures of the con-quered people on that of the conquerors, and thirdly, of the gradual physical mixture of the two peoples. All these factors co-operate in the production of a

[1] Rivers, *Psychology and Politics*, p. 118.

new culture which is neither that of the immigrants nor that of the natives, but a new creation.

Thus the formation of a new culture is not merely an historical phenomenon. It has also a biological aspect, and may be compared in some respects to the formation of a new species. If it is adapted to the environment in which it is placed and to the needs of life that it has to meet, it may persist indefinitely as a stable type. If, on the other hand, it fails to attain this adaptation it will fade away or collapse. In some cases, as in that of the Viking settlers in Greenland, and perhaps also in that of the Maya culture in Central America, the decline of a culture is directly due to its failure to meet the adverse climatic or geographical conditions of its environment. More often, however, the passing of a culture is connected with the disappearance of the immigrant stock through its complete assimilation by the conquered people. This is the normal fate of a conquering aristocracy, and since so many civilizations are the creation of an élite, it is often sufficient to explain the phenomena of stagnation and decline that so often follow a period of brilliant cultural achievement.

This is the factor which Dr. Rivers regarded as all-important for the history of Melanesian society. He showed how the coming of the " Kava-people " in the South and the " Betel-people " in the North brought new types of culture into the Melanesian area, and set up a process of cultural progress which endured until the new elements were completely assimilated by the indigenous population, when society became once more fixed in a stationary and unprogressive type of culture. Nevertheless it must be remembered that the case of Melanesia is not entirely typical; it is an exceptionally backward and outlying region, in which the native tradition of culture was of a rudimentary type. In many cases the conquered people contributes as much as, or even more than, the conquerors to the formation of a new culture. In these cases the period that follows the coming of the new people is a time of cultural decline or stagnation, and the revival of culture is caused by a reassertion of the native element in the culture. This is the origin of those sudden and brilliant revivals of culture such as we see in the Italian Renaissance and in that earlier " Renaissance " of the 6th century B.C. when the Ægean culture awoke to new life after the period of darkness and barbarism that followed the age of the Dorian Invasion.

Thus the culture cycle normally consists of three phases. First comes the period of growth, when the two elements in the culture are not yet fused with one another, and the immigrant people still preserves the cultural tradition that it has brought with it. Secondly there is the period of progress, when the culture, fertilized by the new elements that it has acquired, bursts into flower, and enters on a period of creative activity. And thirdly there is the period of maturity, when either the new elements are completely assimilated and the original culture tradition once more becomes dominant, or when a complete fusion of the two elements takes place and the new type of culture becomes stabilized and permanent.

Hence, in order to judge of the permanence and strength of a culture, we have to consider not only the character of its institutions or the quality of its intellectual achievements, but, before all, its inner vitality. The strength of a political or social institution, like that of an artistic style, depends not on its abstract rationality or beauty, but on its communion with the living culture. The most faithful imitation of an ancient work of art cannot call back to life a vanished style of art when once the living tradition is broken. And just as an artistic or literary fashion can be imitated in an external and artificial way, so, too, can a people adopt the political and social forms of a different culture without having vitally incorporated them. If this process is carried far enough it may involve the end of the living culture, and thus it is possible for an abstract and superficial progress to be the mark of a vital decline.

When the successors of Alexander covered Asia with municipalities, theatres, gymnasia and schools of rhetoric, they did not turn the Asiatics into Greeks, but they did put an end to the native culture traditions, which lingered on only among poor men and country folk. The great network of municipal institutions with which the Hellenistic princes, and afterwards Rome, covered the subject countries were a mechanical and external creation, as compared with the vital and internal impulse that created the Greek City-State. The same thing may be true of representative institutions, universal education, a daily press, and all the other insignia of modern civilization. We have to consider not merely whether an institution is reasonable or good, but first and foremost whether it is alive. There can be no question, for example, but that the modern representative system as it exists on the continent to-day, with its elaborate proportional representation and its universal suffrage, is, in the abstract, highly superior to the English Parliamentary system of the 18th century, with its rotten boroughs, its absurd anomalies of suffrage and its corruption. Yet the latter was the living expression of an age and a people of creative political genius; it was one of the great forces that shaped the modern world; while the former is without a living relation to its society, and is liable to be set aside, as recently in Italy, in favour of a more primitive system which is more deeply rooted in the political traditions of the people. Only so long as change is the spontaneous expression of the society itself does it involve the progress of civilization; as soon as the internal vital development of a culture ceases, change means death.

Anyone looking at the Mediterranean world in the age of Pericles might have thought that the future of humanity was assured. Man seemed at last to have come of age and to have entered into his inheritance. Art, Science and Democracy were all coming to a magnificent flowering in a hundred free cities; and the promise of the future seemed even greater than the achievements of the present. Yet at the very moment when the whole Mediterranean world was ready to embrace the new knowledge and the new ideals of life and art, when the barbarians everywhere were turning to the Hellenic cities as the centre of power and light, all this promise was blighted. Hellenism withered from within. The free cities were torn asunder by mutual hatred and by class wars. They found no place for the greatest minds of the age—perhaps the greatest minds of any age—who were forced to take service with tyrants and kings.

So that at last Hellenic science became domesticated at the court of the Macedonian Pharaohs at Alexandria, and the free cities became the spoil of every successful condottiere.

What was the reason of this sudden blighting of Hellenic civilization? Not, I think, any of the external causes that have been invoked—the Peloponnesian War, the introduction of malaria, the exhaustion of the soil. These were, at most, secondary causes. Nor was it, as Professor Gilbert Murray says in his interesting book on Greek religion, due to a " loss of nerve." It goes deeper than that. Hellenic civilization collapsed not by a failure of nerve but by the failure of life. When Hellenic science was in full flower, the life of the Hellenic world withered from below, and underneath the surface brilliance of philosophy and literature the sources of the life of the people were drying up. The strength of the Hellenic culture rested on a regional and agrarian foundation. The citizen was not only a landowner but a farmer also, and even his religion was inseparable from the family tombs and the shrine of the local hero. In the eyes of the writers of the classical period the typical Greek was not the sophist or the glib Levantine trader, but the rough Acharnian peasant, or the no less rural Dorian noble, the " men who fought at Marathon " and Platæa. But in the two centuries between the Persian War and the Hellenistic period the Greeks had ceased to be an agricultural people and had become a nation of town dwellers. The countryside was depopulated, and the land was cultivated by slave labour, while the citizen class, decimated in civil war and political revolutions, had drifted into the cities or emigrated to the newly-conquered lands of the East.

As the life passed out of Hellenic civilization, we see the gradual disappearance of those vital characteristic types in which the spirit of the culture had embodied itself, the passing away of the traditional institutions and the fading of the vivid and highly differentiated life of the regional city-state into a formless, cosmopolitan society, with no roots in the past and no contact with a particular region, a society which was common to the great cities everywhere from Mesopotamia to the Bay of Naples. Hence the degradation of the Greek type. The people is no longer represented by the citizen-soldier, who brought down the power of Persia, but by the " starveling Greek " of Juvenal's satire, the Jack-of-all-Trades from rhetoric to rope-dancing. Instead of the Hellene being by nature the master and the barbarian the slave, we have Persius' centurion, " big Vulfenius," who, " with a guffaw, offers a bad halfpenny for a hundred Greeks."

Yet throughout the period of this vital decline, the intellectual achievements of Hellenic civilization remained, and Greek culture, in an abstract and standardized form, was spreading East and West far more than it had done in the days of its living strength.

If intellectual progress—or at least a high degree of scientific achievement—can co-exist with vital decline, if a civilization can fall to pieces from within—then the optimistic assumptions of the last two centuries concerning the future of our modern civilization lose their validity. The fate of the Hellenic world is a warning to us that the higher and the more intellectually

66

advanced civilizations of the West may be inferior in point of survival value to the more rudimentary Oriental cultures.

For there is a vital difference between the fixation or stagnation of a civilization like that of China or Egypt, after the close of its formative and progressive culture cycle, and the organic dissolution of a culture, such as we see in the case of ancient Greece and Rome. The cultures of China and Egypt survived for thousands of years because they preserved their foundations intact. By their fixed and hieratic ordering of social relations they gave to the simplest and humblest functions all the consecration of religion and tradition. But the classical civilizations neglected the roots of their life in a premature concentration on power or wealth, so that their temporary conquest of the world was paid for by the degeneration and perhaps the destruction of their own social organs.

This is an extreme example of the perils that result from the urbanization of a culture, but a similar process can be traced in many other cases of social decline.

First comes the concentration of culture in the city, with a great resultant heightening of cultural activity. But this is followed by the lowering of the level of culture in the country and the widening of the gulf between townsman and peasant. In some cases, as in ancient Greece, this amounts to a gradual but thorough rebarbarization of the country, in others—as in Russia since Peter the Great, and in the Hellenistic East since Alexander—the peasants still cling to the traditions of a native culture, while the towns adopt a ready-made urban civilization from abroad. In the last stage the cities lose all economic and vital contact with the region in which they are placed. They have become parasitic; less dependent on nature and more dependent on the maintenance of an artificial political and economic system.

It is this process of urban degeneration which is one of the greatest sources of weakness in our modern European Culture. Our civilization is becoming formless and moribund because it has lost its roots and no longer possesses vital rhythm and balance.

The rawness and ugliness of modern European life is the sign of biological inferiority, of an insufficient or false relation to environment, which produces strain, wasted effort, revolt or failure. Just as a mechanical, industrial civilization will seek to eliminate all waste movements in work, so as to make the operative the perfect complement of his machine, so a vital civilization will cause every function and every act to partake of vital grace and beauty. To a great extent this is entirely instinctive, as in the grace of the old agricultural operations, ploughing, sowing and reaping, but it is also the goal of conscious effort in the great Oriental cultures—as in the caligraphy of the Moslem scribe, and the elaboration of Oriental social etiquette. Why is a stockbroker less beautiful than a Homeric warrior or an Egyptian priest? Because he is less incorporated with life; he is not inevitable, but accidental, almost parasitic. When a culture has proved its real needs and organized its vital functions, every office becomes beautiful. So, too, with dress, the full Victorian panoply of top hat and frock coat undoubtedly expressed something essential in the 19th century culture, and hence it has spread with that culture all over the world as no fashion of clothing has ever done before. It is possible that our descendants will recognize in it a kind of grim and Assyrian beauty, fit emblem of the ruthless and great age that created it; but, however that may be, it misses the direct and inevitable beauty that all clothing should have, because, like its parent-culture, it was out of touch with the life of nature and of human nature as well.

No civilization, however advanced, can afford to neglect these ultimate foundations in the life of nature and the natural region on which its social welfare depends, for even the highest achievements of science and art and economic organization are powerless to avert decay, if the vital functions of the social organism become impaired. Apparent progress is often accompanied by a process of social degeneration or decomposition, which destroys the stability of a civilization, but, as Le Play insisted, this process is not an inevitable one. However far the process of degeneration has gone, there is always a possibility of regeneration, if society recovers its functional equilibrium and restores its lost contacts with the life of nature.

IV

THE COMPARATIVE STUDY OF RELIGIONS AND THE SPIRITUAL ELEMENT IN CULTURE

WE have seen in the last chapter that culture, even in its highest forms, is ultimately dependent on and conditioned by physical factors. Man, like every other form of animal life, is the creature of environment, heredity and function, and consequently his culture is not an abstract intellectual construction, but a material organization of life, which is submitted to the same laws of growth and decay, of " generation and corruption," as the rest of the material world.

It might seem at first sight as though this leads to a completely determinist conception of history which will leave no room for rational purpose or the free co-operation of the human mind. And this is certainly the logical conclusion of the Spenglerian view of culture which subordinates human intelligence and freedom to the cyclical working of a blind law of destiny. Still more, if we accept the postulates of the old scientific materialism, we must regard the intellectual and spiritual aspects of culture as secondary and derivative. The vital process of culture would be as purely physical as the process of digestion, and the reasons and emotions that seem to govern it would be no more causative than the feeling of pleasure which accompanies the assimilation of food is the cause of bodily nutrition.

Yet, as we have already seen, the materialists themselves have been slow to draw this apparently obvious conclusion. Actually they did not attempt to reduce human life to a purely instinctive activity, or to underestimate the part played by human reason in social development. It is true that during the last thirty years the reaction to the excessive intellectualism of idealist philosophy has produced a similar exaggeration in the opposite direction, and there has been a tendency to minimize the importance of the rational element in human life. Nevertheless all such attempts are only partial in their scope, and affect the problem of origins rather than the validity of results. The Behaviourist may describe thought as suppressed speech, and speech as suppressed gesture, the psychoanalyst may see in the most ideal aspirations the secret working of a repressed sexual complex, but each of them implicitly admits the possibility of some rationalizing of experience, since he would otherwise destroy the claims of his own theory to explain facts at all.

Again there is no one who will deny that our modern way of life has been profoundly affected by machinery, that machinery presupposes the science of mechanics, and that mechanics are impossible without mathematics; and if this is so, it is impossible to deny that action may be affected by thought at other stages of the cultural process. However far we may go back in the history of humanity we shall still find room for the modification of human life by thought and

71

invention. The discovery of agriculture and the domestication of animals transformed human culture no less radically than the coming of the new techniques of science and industry. And at the still earlier stage —at the dawn of humanity—there were those great primitive discoveries of the use of fire, of tools, and weapons, and clothing, which prepared the way for man's subsequent conquest of nature.

Nor can we suppose that these practical inventions were the first or the only manifestation of a specifically human activity. If man is essentially a tool-using animal, the tool is from the beginning that of the artist, no less than that of the labourer. Already, ages before man had learned to build houses, to cultivate the ground, or to domesticate animals, he was an artist of no mean order, as we know from the remains of the magnificent cave-paintings of palæolithic times. But the art of the primitive is not merely an indulgence of the æsthetic instinct, it has a severely practical—one might even say rational—purpose. Its purpose is not to give pleasure or to reproduce what a man sees, but to exert man's power over external nature. Thus in all probability the animal paintings of the palæolithic period were conceived as the magical means by which the primitive hunter put a spell upon his prey and acquired the power to overcome the strength and cunning of the wild animals. And among peoples of lower culture to-day, such as the negroes, and the natives of Australia or Melanesia, art is almost without exception the outward expression of a strict ritual or ceremonial tradition that governs the whole life of a people. Early explorers and ethnologists were apt to suppose that the more uncivilized peoples lived an almost entirely material existence occupied only with the satisfaction of their material needs. "He thinks of nothing except the matters that immediately concern his daily material needs," is a typical remark quoted by Herbert Spencer in his reconstruction of primitive mentality.[1] But a more intimate knowledge of the life of primitive peoples gives a very different impression. A people like the Australians, whose material culture is the barest imaginable, and who were regarded by the early European settlers as utterly devoid of religion or morality, and hardly above the level of the beasts, are now known to possess a wealth of ceremonial which surpasses in elaboration the religious practices of many advanced peoples. Their ceremonies often extend over months, and determine the whole rhythm of social life by supplying the chief incentive to organized work and social activity.

So far indeed is the Central Australian native from that preoccupation with immediate bodily needs which is regarded by Herbert Spencer as characteristic of primitive mentality, that the most important part of his life is that which is devoted to ceremonial observances. His thoughts are centred, not on the concerns of the present life, but on the mysterious dream world of the Alcheringa, the home of the totemic ancestors—the fathers and creators of the world of man. Thus Spencer and Gillen write: "From the moment of initiation his life is sharply marked out into two parts. He has first of all what we may speak of as the ordinary life, common to all the men and women, and associated with the procuring of food and the performances of corrobborees. . . .

[1] *The Principles of Sociology*, I, p. 79.

73

On the other hand, he has what gradually becomes of greater and greater importance to him, and that is the portion of his life devoted to matters of a sacred or secret nature. As he grows older he takes an increasing share in these, until finally this side of his life occupies by far the greater part of his thoughts. The sacred ceremonies, which appear very trivial matters to the white man, are most serious matters to him. They are all connected with the great ancestors of the tribe, and he is firmly convinced that when it comes to his turn to die, his spirit part will finally return to his old *alcheringa* home, where he will be in communion with them until such time as it seems good to him to undergo reincarnation."[1]

Now it is obvious that this elaborate growth of ceremonial and belief cannot be deduced simply from the influences of the Australian environment and the material needs of savage life. It is conditioned by them, but it has an independent origin and history which might have followed a different course, even though the racial and geographical conditions remained unaltered. Nor can we believe that this development was, as Durkheim maintained, a purely collective one in which the individual consciousness was entirely merged in that of the crowd. It is impossible to exclude the factor of individual thought and leadership from any stage of religious development. The influence of the exceptional man—we may even say of the genius— whether as organizer, teacher, or seer, is to be observed among savages no less than in advanced civilizations, and the fact that a primitive culture, such as that

[1] B. Spencer and F. J. Gillen, *The Northern Tribes of Central Australia*, 1904, pp. 33-4.

74

of the Central Australians, may become fixed in a Byzantine rigidity of ritual formalism does not exclude the possibility that it once passed through a formative period in which it received the impress of individual creative minds.

It is this inner aspect of a culture which constitutes its most distinctive features. The unity of a culture rests not only on a community of place—the common environment, a community of work—the common function, and a community of blood—the common race, it springs also, and above all, from a community of thought. For a culture even of the most rudimentary kind is never simply a material unity. It involves not only a certain uniformity in social organization and in the way of life, but also a continuous and conscious social discipline. Even a common language, which is essential for any kind of social life, can only be evolved by centuries of co-operative rational effort. Here ages of thinking and acting in common have produced a terminology, a system of classification and even a scale of values which in turn impose themselves on the minds of all who come under its influence, so as to justify the old saying that a new language is a new soul. But it is not only in this way that the common thought of a society finds expression. There is also a common conception of reality, a view of life, which even in the most primitive societies expresses itself through magical practices and religious beliefs, and which in the higher cultures appears in a fuller and more conscious form in religion, science and philosophy. In this way the intellectual factor conditions the development of every society. It is the active and creative element in culture, since it emancipates man from the purely biological

75

laws which govern the development of animal species, and enables him to accumulate a growing capital of knowledge and social experience, which gives him a progressive control over his material environment.

It is true that it is never independent of the latter, since the intellectual element in a culture is consubstantial with its material substratum, in the same way that the mind of the individual is consubstantial with his body. But just as the individual mind infuses the body, so too is the intellectual element the soul and the formative principle of a culture. Two peoples may possess a common geographical environment and a common racial type and yet differ entirely in culture if they do not share the same intellectual tradition. We have seen whole countries pass from one culture to another without any fundamental change of population, and again, in the case of Islam, we see a new attitude to life, which first arose in the arid plateau of Arabia, transforming the lives and social organization of the Slavonic mountaineers of Bosnia, the Malay pirate of the East Indies, the highly civilized city dwellers of Persia and Northern India, and the barbarous negro tribes of Africa. The ultimate barriers between peoples are not those of race or language or region, but those differences of spiritual outlook and tradition which are seen in the contrast of Hellene and Barbarian, Jew and Gentile, Moslem and Hindu, Christian and Pagan. In all such cases there is a different conception of reality, different moral and æsthetic standards, in a word, a different inner world. Behind every civilization there is a vision—a vision which may be the unconscious fruit of ages of common thought and action, or which may have sprung from the sudden illumination of a great prophet or thinker. The experience of Mohammed in the cave of Mount Hira, when he saw human life as transitory as the beat of a gnat's wing in comparison with the splendour and power of the Divine Unity, has shaped the existence of a great part of the human race ever since. For a people which has heard thrice a day for a thousand years the voice of the muezzin proclaiming the unity of God cannot live the same life or see with the same eyes as the Hindu who worships the life of nature in its countless forms, and sees the external world as a manifestation of the interplay of cosmic sexual forces.

But while an intellectual or spiritual change will produce far-reaching reactions upon the material culture of a people, a purely external or material change will produce little positive effect unless it has some root in the psychic life of a culture. It is well known that the influence of the material civilization of modern Europe on a primitive people does not normally lead to cultural progress. On the contrary, unless it is accompanied by a gradual process of education and spiritual assimilation it will destroy the culture that it has conquered. A people can only utilize new knowledge or new techniques if they are brought into relation with the spirit of their culture and their general attitude to life. An interesting example of this has recently been recorded of a tribe in Papua who had been brought into contact with wireless telegraphy. Their minds were so powerfully affected by the invention that they attempted to imitate it, and produced a complete model of a wireless aerial and masts. But they transformed its purpose in accordance with the dominant idea of their own culture, and used it as a method of entering into communication with the spirits of the dead. Thus the latest triumph of European science became in their hands simply a new addition to the magical technique of the native culture tradition.

The vital changes in culture are those that come from within, and consequently the greatest of all agents of cultural progress is the human mind. This may seem at first sight to be a return to the old intellectualist view of progress which inspired the philosophers and sociologists of the 18th and 19th centuries and which was discussed in Chapter I. But men like Helvetius, Condorcet, and Buckle, conceived the rational element in history in a very different sense from that which we are here suggesting. For example, Buckle regards the increase of knowledge and scientific discovery as all-important, and excludes morals, religion, literature, and government from any vital influence on social progress. They are the results of a culture, not its causes. He even goes so far as to maintain that the discovery of gunpowder has done more to promote the cause of peace than all the preaching of Christianity!

In reality it is easy to see that scientific knowledge and the spirit of rational criticism, though they have had a vast influence on the recent development of our own civilization are of very limited importance in other ages and cultures. If we are to estimate the importance of the intellectual element in culture, we must extend the conception of mind to include the whole domain of human consciousness from the first obscure effort to correlate the data of sensible experience up to the highest achievements of the speculative intellect.

The process of reducing the unintelligible multiplicity and heterogeneity of the sensible world to order and unity is co-extensive with the history of humanity. It is never completed since there is an irreducible element that escapes the utmost efforts of science and philosophy, but on the other hand it has been in progress ever since man first began to give names to things and to classify and arrange his experience through language. From the very dawn of primitive culture men have attempted, in however crude and symbolic a form, to understand the laws of life and to adapt their social activity to their workings. But primitive man does not look upon the external world in the modern way, as a passive or mechanistic system, a background for human energies, mere matter for the human mind to mould. He sees it as a living world of mysterious forces, greater than his own, in the placation and service of which his life consists. And the first need of a people, no less important than food or weapons, is the psychical equipment or technique by which man is enabled to enter into communication with these superhuman powers and cause them to be propitious to him. As Durkheim has said, religion is like the womb from which come all the germs of human civilization. " Since it has been made to embrace all of reality, the physical world as well as the moral one, the forces that move bodies as well as those that move minds have been conceived in a religious form. That is how the most diverse methods and practices, both those that make possible the continuation of the moral life (laws, morals and art) and those serving the material life (the material, technical and practical sciences) are directly or indirectly derived from religion." "From the moment when men have an idea that there are internal connections between things science and philosophy become possible. Religion opened the way for them."[1]

The reason of this, however, is not as Durkheim would have us believe, that religion is nothing else but the divinization of the social consciousness. On the contrary, though social life is dependent on religion, the sphere of religion is that which lies outside social control, and the primary religious instinct is that of dependence on superhuman powers. This sense is even stronger in primitive man than among the peoples of higher culture, since the latter always possess a certain autonomy in relation to the external world, while the savage lives in a state of permanent dependence on forces which he can neither understand nor control. He is surrounded by mysterious powers which manifest themselves both in external nature and in his inner consciousness, in earth and sky, in beasts and plants, no less than in dreams and visions and in the spirits of the dead. Hence primitive religion is characterized by its universality and vagueness and it is impossible to isolate a single definite type of religious belief and practice as the source and starting point of the whole development.

Modern writers on anthropology and primitive thought have tended to assume that religion is a secondary phenomenon and that man's earliest attitude to reality was a kind of empirical materialism. Thus the classical theory of the evolutionary school of

[1] E. Durkheim, *The Elementary Forms of the Religious Life* (Eng. tr.), pp. 223, 237.

anthropologists from Tylor to Frazer ascribe the origin of religion to a superstitious dread of ghosts, which was gradually extended from the spirits of the dead, so that every strange or terrible phenomenon in nature was regarded as the work of similar personal spirits. Hence, in Tylor's words, the conception of a human soul served as the model for man's ideas of spiritual beings in general "from the tiniest elf which sports in the long grass up to the heavenly Creator and Ruler of the World—the Great Spirit."[1]

This explanation seemed to afford a simple key to the whole process of religious evolution, and it is easy to understand how attractive it must have been to the contemporaries of Darwin and Herbert Spencer. But a more detailed study of primitive cultures has shown that it is impossible to isolate a single belief or even a particular type of beliefs as the source and starting point of religious development. The whole mentality of primitive man is religious, and the belief in personal spirits is but one aspect of his thought. His conception of reality is never limited to that which he sees and touches. So far from being a materialist, it is, as Mary Kingsley said, an effort to him to think in terms of matter. "His mind works along the line that things happen because of the action of spirit upon spirit. We think upon the line that things happen from the action of matter upon matter. . . . The Englishman is constrained by circumstances to perceive the existence of an (external) material world. The African regards spirit and matter as undivided in kind, matter being only the extreme low form of spirit."[2]

---

[1] E. B. Tylor, *Primitive Culture*, II, pp. 109 ff.
[2] M. Kingsley, *West African Studies*, p. 330 (2nd ed.).

Among the more advanced peoples of primitive culture this conception of the spiritual nature of reality attains almost philosophical expression. Thus a Dakota priest explained to Mr. James Walker that the forms we see are not the real forms but only their tonwapi— i.e. the manifestation of the divine power that possesses them. For every object in the world has a spirit and that spirit is Wakan—the divine power—which comes from Wakan beings that are greater than mankind, just as mankind is greater than the animals. Even more remarkable is the belief of the Maoris that the outer world is the aria or reflection of the gods. Mr. Elsdon Best relates that a missionary told a Maori that his religion was false since it taught that everything had a soul. Whereupon the Maori answered: " Were a thing not possessed by the wairua of an atua—the shadow of a god—that thing could not have form." What enables us to know a material object is not its physical nature but the spirit that possesses it. Moreover, every being possesses an eternal element—" the toiora of the enduring world " —and the toiora of the universe is nothing else but the soul of the supreme god—IO, the Self-Determined.[1]

These ideas are not, of course, representative of primitive man. They seem to represent the most advanced type of speculation that is to be found among any peoples of the lower culture. Nevertheless they do but render explicit the view of reality which exists in a confused and vague form among all primitive peoples. Everywhere we find the belief that there exists behind the outward appearance of things a

[1] P. Radin, *Primitive Man as Philosopher*, pp. 252-5.

mysterious world of spiritual or supernatural forces, which rule the course of nature and the life of man.

Among the more advanced peoples these forces are conceived in a more personal and individualized form as spiritual beings, such as the " Masters " or " Owners " of the Palæo-Siberian peoples, the Guardian spirits of the Indians of the Plains, and the departmental nature gods of the polytheistic peoples all over the world. But there is also a less developed form of primitive religion which conceives the supernatural power behind the world as a vast undifferentiated unity. Even the Koryak of Siberia who conceive their deity in a more or less personal form, name him not only " The Master on High " or " The Thunder Man," but also " The Universe " or " The Outer One," " That which Exists " and " Existence " or " Strength." In Africa the Yok of the Lango, the Mulungu of the Yao, and the Engai of the Masai, to take only a few examples, is not so much the title of a God as the name for the undifferentiated supernatural power which shows itself at once in magic, in the operations of nature, and in the spirits of the dead.

But it is among the hunting peoples of North America that this conception of a vague supernatural power diffused throughout nature has attained its most definite expression under such names as the Orenda of the Iroquois, the Wakan of the Sioux, the Algonquian Manito, the Athabascan Coen and the Yok of the Tlingit. Thus Swanton writes of the Tlingit Indians in Alaska: " The Tlingit do not divide the universe arbitrarily into so many different quarters ruled by so many supernatural beings. On the contrary, supernatural power impresses them as a vast immensity, one in kind and impersonal, inscrutable as to its nature, but whenever manifesting itself to men taking a personal, and it might be said a human personal form in whatever aspect it displays itself. Thus the sky spirit is the ocean of supernatural energy as it manifests itself in the sky, the sea spirit as it manifests itself in the sea, the bear spirit as it manifests itself in the bear, the rock spirit as it manifests itself in the rock, etc. It is not meant that the Tlingit consciously reasons this out, or formulates a unity in the supernatural, but such appears to be his unexpressed feeling. For this reason there is but one name for this spiritual power, Yok, a name which is affixed to any specific manifestation of it, and it is to this perception or feeling reduced to personality, that the 'Great Spirit' idea seems usually to have affixed itself.

"This supernatural energy must be carefully differentiated from natural energy and never confused with it. It is true that the former is supposed to bring about results similar to the latter, but in the mind of the Tlingit the conceived difference between the two is as great as with us. A rock rolling downhill or an animal running is by no means a manifestation of supernatural energy, although if something peculiar be associated with these actions, something outside the Indian's usual experience of such phenomena, they may be thought of as such."[1] Again a Dakota chief gave the following explanation of the Indian belief to Miss Alice Fletcher.[2] " Everything as it moves now and then, here and there makes stops. A

[1] J. R. Swanton, *Social Conditions, Beliefs and Linguistic Relations of the Tlingit Indian*, in 26th Annual Report of Bureau of American Ethnology, pp. 451-2, note.
[2] Peabody Museum Report, vol. III, p. 276, note.

84

bird as it flies stops in one place to make its nest and in another place to rest from its flight. A man when he goes forth stops when he wills. So the god (Wakan) has stopped. The sun, which is so bright and beautiful, is one place where he has stopped. The moon, the stars, the winds he has been with. The trees, the animals, are all where he has stopped, and the Indian thinks of these places and sends his prayers to reach where the god has stopped and to win health and a blessing."

Now this vague conception of an " ocean of super-natural energy " is not one that it is easy for primitive or even civilized man to define or express. It forms the background of his whole thought and view of life, but for that very reason it escapes the eye of the superficial observer. Thus it is not surprising that the missionary, the traveller and the anthropologist have derived their ideas of the religion of primitive peoples from the myths and folk tales which belong rather to the foreground of the social consciousness. Thus in the case of the Tlingit, the obvious feature of their religions will appear to be not that diffused super-natural power of which we have spoken, but a perfectly definite character Yehl the Raven, whose comic and often most unedifying exploits are the subject of countless tales and who is also a kind of demiurge and culture-hero who brought fire to men and set the sun and the stars in their places in heaven. Never-theless these rationalistic and apparently irreverent myths are somehow reconcilable with a profoundly religious attitude of mind. Among the Bushmen, for instance, we have Cagn the Mantis, a trickster like Yehl the Raven or Reynard the Fox, who married the Hyrax and adopted the Porcupine as his daughter. Yet J. M. Orpen records the following words of a Bushman hunter, Quing, " Cagn made all things and we pray to him, ' O Cagn, O Cagn, are we not your children? Do not you see our hunger? Give us food.' Where Cagn is, Quing did not know, but the elands know. Have you not hunted and heard his cry, when the elands suddenly run to his call? "

The fact is, as Andrew Lang pointed out, that mythology and religion in the strict sense of the word are two different things which have become inextricably entangled with one another, but are quite distinct in origin. It is, however, doubtful whether Lang was right in ascribing the origins of myth to the tendency of the primitive mind to find an explanation for every natural phenomenon—how the leopard got his spots, why the moon wanes and so forth, in the manner of the " Just So Stories." For an American scholar, T. T. Waterman, has shown that, at least in North America, the diffusion of a myth is usually wider than that of the explanation which has become attached to it, and therefore he concludes that the explanatory element is secondary.[1]

It is, however, easy enough to understand how, when once a story has become popular, it may be given cosmological significance, and even attached to the shadowy divine beings of the religious pantheon, so that the attributes of a typical trickster, such as Old Man Coyote in North America may become interchanged with those of a purely religious figure, like the Sun. Thus the two conceptions of Cagn the Creator and Cagn the Trickster may have belonged

[1] T. T. Waterman, in the *Journal of American Folklore*, vol. 27, 1914, pp. 1-54·

originally to two different departments of thought which were ultimately fused together by becoming attached to the sacred insect, the Mantis.

Hence Andrew Lang was completely justified in maintaining that mythology was almost devoid of religious significance. Indeed, this is sometimes clearly admitted by the primitive peoples themselves. For example the Omaha and kindred tribes draw a sharp distinction between the myths and stories and the sacred rites and visions. The former are mere legends or " lying tales," and are described as " pertaining to the ludicrous." The latter, on the other hand, could only be approached with prayer and fasting. They were " pertaining to Wakanda " or the supernatural. A similar division seems to have been made by the Pueblo Indians.[1]

Mythology belongs to a different world from that of religious experience, and the absurdities and grotesqueness of the former are no argument against the depth and reality of the latter. Professor Lowie describes the central figure of the cosmological myths of the Crow Indians as a typical trickster " wallowing in grossness and buffoonery." And yet at the same time " the Crow Indian approached the universe with a sincere humility that contrasted sharply with his personal pride towards fellow-tribesmen. He evinced that sense of absolute dependence on something not himself which Schleiermacher and Feuerbach postulate as the root of the religious sentiment. By himself man was nothing, but somewhere in the world there were mysterious beings greater than he, by

---

[1] J. Dorsey, *A Study of Siouan Cults*, pp. 368-9. 11th Annual Report of Bureau of Ethnology, Washington, 1889-90.

whose good will he might rise."[1] What could be more profoundly religious than the song of the Pawnee warrior.

> "Oh you who possess the skies.
> I am living. I in you entrust my fate
> Again alone upon the war path."

And yet this attitude, which has no lack of expression in primitive prayer and ritual, finds nothing to justify it in mythology.

As one of the early French missionaries in Canada wrote: "To speak truth these peoples have derived from their fathers no knowledge of a god, and before we set foot in their country they had nothing but vain fables about the origin of the world. Nevertheless, savages as they were, there did abide in their hearts a secret sentiment of a divinity, and of a first principle, author of all things, whom, not knowing they yet invoked. In the forest, in the chase, on the water, in peril by sea, they call him to their aid."[2]

Nevertheless mythology has its own value and importance, if not in the sphere of religion at least in that of thought. It gives room for the first exercise of free rational enquiry and opens the way to genuine intellectual speculation which finds expression in the elaborate semi-philosophical cosmological systems of the Polynesians and the Pueblo Indians. Even in its more primitive forms it embodies a certain criticism of life. Indeed it may be argued that the omnipresent figure of the trickster is given the leading place in cosmology, not merely for his literary attractiveness,

[1] R. H. Lowie, *Primitive Religion*, pp. 21 and 18.
[2] Père Lallemant, *Relation*, 1648, p. 77, in A. Lang *Myth, Ritual and Religion*, II, 68.

but because primitive man is conscious of an arbitrary and malevolent element in life which must have a wider cosmic significance. Among the African peoples, above all, the existence of a critical and pessimistic attitude to life is especially marked. The divine figures of mythology are not merely ·cunning tricksters, they are often definitely malevolent powers who lie in wait for man to destroy him. Or they are beings which have changed their original nature and hardened their hearts towards man. " Cagn at first was very good and nice, but he got spoilt through fighting so many things," said the same Bushman Quing whom we have already quoted. " Leza, the god of the Ba Ila, is not only the creator and preserver who sends rain and fruitful seasons. He is the Besetting One, he who sits on the back of every one of us and we cannot shake him off." Like Cagn, he has become old and perverse, and the whole order of nature has become changed for the worse.[1]

It seems as though the critical element in primitive thought does not as a rule tend towards the advancement and purification of religious conceptions, but rather to their contamination and negation.

The dynamic element in primitive culture is to be found rather in the sphere of direct religious experience than in that of conscious rational enquiry. It may seem paradoxical to suggest that the starting point of human progress is to be found in the highest type of knowledge—the intuition of pure being, but it must be remembered that intellectually, at least, man's development is not so much from the lower to the

---

[1] E. W. Smith and A. M. Dale, *The Ila Speaking Peoples of Northern Rhodesia* (1920), vol. II, pp. 197 ff.

higher as from the confused to the distinct. Art and literature, for example, do not advance in the same continuous line of development that we find in material culture. A "low" culture can produce an art which is in its kind perfect and incapable of improvement. In the same way even the most backward peoples possess a highly developed religious sense which at times expresses itself with an almost mystical intensity. The ultimate foundation of primitive religion is not a belief in ghosts or mythical beings, but an obscure and confused intuition of transcendent being—an "ocean of supernatural energy," "pelagus substantiae infinitum et indeterminatum."

He is neither an animist nor a polytheist, since the mysterious power he worships is not completely identified with any of the individual forms through which it is manifested. Nor is he a pantheist, since the essential quality of this power is its transcendent or supernatural character.

"The religious faith of the Dakota is not in his gods as such. It is in a mysterious and intangible something of which they are only the embodiment, and that in such a measure and degree as may accord with the individual fancy of the worshipper. Each one will worship some of these divinities and neglect and despise others; but the great object of all their worship, whatever its chosen medium, is the Taku Wakan, which is the supernatural and mysterious. No one term can express the full meaning of the Dakota's Wakan. It comprehends all mystery, secret power and divinity."[1]

[1] Riggs in J. Dorsey, *Study of Siouan Cults*, p. 432-3. 11th Annual Report of Bureau of Ethnology, Washington, 1889-90.

Thus alike for the savage and the philosopher all ends in mystery, and the vagueness and confusion of the primitive mind reaches the same conclusion as the profundity of the mystic who wrote

Καὶ πάντων τέλος ἐσσὶ, καὶ εἷς καὶ πάντα καὶ οὐδείς,
οὐχ ἕν ἐών, οὐ πάντα——πανώνυμε, πῶς σε καλέσω,
τὸν μόνον ἀκλήϊστον.[1]

[1] The End of all art Thou, being One and All and None,
Being One Thou art not all, being All thou art not one,
All names are Thine, how then shall I invoke Thy Name
Alone Indefinite.

St. Gregory Nazianzen.
ὕμνος εἰς θεΐν.

91

PART II

V

RELIGION AND THE ORIGINS OF CIVILIZATION

IF the rational and spiritual elements in a culture
are those which determine its creative activity, and
if the primary manifestation of these elements is to
be found in the sphere of religion, it is clear that the
religious factor has had a far more important share
in the development of human cultures than that
which has been usually assigned to it by the theorists
who have attempted to explain the phenomena of
social progress.

Ever since the rise of the modern scientific movement in the 18th century there has been a tendency
among sociologists and historians of culture to neglect
the study of religion in its fundamental social aspects.
As we have seen, the apostles of the 18th century
Enlightenment were, above all, intent on deducing
the laws of social life and progress from a small number
of simple rational principles. They hacked through
the luxuriant and deep-rooted growth of traditional
belief with the ruthlessness of pioneers in a tropical
jungle. They felt no need to understand the development of the historic religions or their influence on
the course of human history, for to them historic
religion was essentially a negative force like ignorance

or tyranny. With Condorcet they found a sufficient explanation of its existence in the duplicity of the first knave and the simplicity of the first fool.

And in the 19th century, apart from the St. Simonian circle, the same attitude, expressed, it is true, with less frankness and brutality, still dominated scientific thought, and found classical expression in England in the culture history of Buckle and in the sociology of Herbert Spencer. Indeed to-day, in spite of the reaction of the last thirty years, it has largely become a part of our intellectual heritage, and is taken for granted in much current sociology and anthropology.

Religion was conceived of as a complex of ideas and speculations concerning the Unknowable, and thus belonged to a different world from that which was the province of sociology. The social progress, which the latter science studies, is the result of the direct response of man to his material environment, and to the growth of positive knowledge concerning the material world. Thus social evolution is a unity which can be studied without reference to the numerous changing systems of religious belief and practice that have risen and fallen during its course. The latter may reflect in some degree the cultural circumstances under which they have arisen, but they are secondary, and in no sense a formative element in the production of culture.

And undoubtedly these ideas held good for the age in which they were formed. During the 18th and 19th centuries the world of secular culture was an autonomous kingdom, whose progress owed nothing to the beliefs and sanctions of the existing authoritative religion. But it is dangerous to argue back from the highly specialized conditions of an advanced and complicated civilization to the elementary principles of social development. Indeed it needs but a moment's thought to realize that that extraordinary age of intellectual political and economic revolution is comparable with no other period in the history of the world. It was at once creative and destructive, but essentially transitional and impermanent, and this instability was due to no other cause than to that very separation and dislocation of the inner and outer worlds of human experience which the thinkers of the age accepted as a normal condition of existence.

In the case of primitive culture, above all, no such dualism existed. The whole life of society had a religious orientation, and religion was the vital centre of the social organism. This is not because primitive man is essentially more religious than modern man, or less interested in the material side of life. It is because the material and spiritual aspects of his culture are inextricably intermingled with one another, as that the religious factor intervenes at every moment of his existence. Even the simplest of his material needs can only be satisfied by the favour or the co-operation of supernatural forces. In the words of a Red Indian: "No man can succeed in life alone, and he cannot get the help he needs from men." He turns to religion not only to obtain spiritual goods such as knowledge or bravery, but also for success in the chase, for health and fecundity, for rain and for the fruits of the earth. Above all, the moments of vital change in the life of the individual—birth, puberty and death—are pre-eminently religious, for the dangerous and difficult passage from one state of existence to another brings man into closer contact with the supernatural, and it is only by the help of religious rites that he can safely pass through the ordeal. But apart from exceptional crises, such as these, man feels the need, even in normal times, of recurring to the help of the higher powers, and of bringing his ordinary existence into contact with and under the sanctions of that other world of mysterious and sacred potencies whose action he always conceives as the ultimate and fundamental law of life.

Hence the most important figure in primitive society is the man who is supposed to be in contact with this other world and to possess supernatural powers. According to the old *a priori* theory of human evolution, brute force was the law of primitive society, and the human pack was ruled and led by the strongest human animal, while the weak went to the wall. But this theory is not borne out by the evidence of facts. Selfishness and brute force are far less predominant in savage life than we should expect, and the weak often fare better than is the case in civilized society. For example, an authority on the Andaman Islands writes : " Every care and consideration are paid by all classes to the very young, the weak, the aged, and the helpless, and these, being made special objects of interest and attention, often fare better in regard to the comforts and necessaries of daily life than any of the otherwise more fortunate members of the community."[1]

So, too, the man who is held in highest honour in primitive society is not the man who possesses

[1] E. H. Man in *J.R.A.I.*, XII, p. 93. " In the same way children are almost always treated with extreme indulgence by primitive peoples, and corporal

physical strength or skill in the chase or even prowess in war, but the dreamer and the mystic. All over the world, and especially among the most backward and primitive peoples, the men who are held to have undergone some supernatural experience are regarded as consecrated and set apart from their fellows. In most cases they form an organized class or profession, indeed they afford the earliest example of social differentiation in primitive society.

Such are the Shamans of Siberia, the Angakok of the Eskimo, the Medicine Men of North America, the Oko-jumu or "Dreamers" of the Andaman Islands, and the Nganga or Diviners among the Bantu peoples. The essential feature of the institution is always the possession of supernatural knowledge or powers which are acquired either through trance or ecstasy or by means of dream visions. The phenomena of trance are most highly developed among the Siberian peoples, and consequently the name of Shamanism is generally applied to the whole development. There is indeed a remarkable similarity in the psycho-physical manifestations of this visionary experience in different parts of the world. The Zulu Inyanga, no less than the Siberian Shaman or the Australian magician passes through a period of profound mental and physical disturbance before acquiring full supernatural powers. He becomes a "house of dreams." "His body becomes turbid," and he can neither sleep nor eat. Even if he turns aside from

---

punishment is almost unknown." Moreover the whole system of social discipline is often very mild. C. Wissler writes of the American Indians: "The whole control of the local group in aboriginal days seems to have been exercised by admonition and mild ridicule instead of by force and punishment."—*The American Indian*, p. 189.

99

his vocation and gets a great doctor to lay the spirit so that he no longer divines, he remains all his life different from his fellows.[1]

Since anything wonderful and outside the common order of things is regarded as supernatural, every kind of psychopathic phenomenon is apt to be associated with Shamanism. But the institution covers a much wider field. Every exceptional man tends to become a Shaman, and consequently he may be a man of outstanding powers of mind and of genuine inspiration or merely an unstable neurotic personality or a trickster and conjuror. So, too, in different regions the office of the Shaman may become specialized, as that of a healer and exorcist, as a prophet and diviner or as a conjuror and miracle worker. Among the Arctic peoples, the well-known phenomena of spiritualism takes the leading place, and the Shaman is not unlike our Western mediums. In North America, on the other hand, the Shaman is often a prophet who leads his people in times of social crisis, for as Mooney has observed in his study of the Ghost Dance Religion among the Sioux, all the great tribal movements of North America may be traced to the teaching of some prophets who claimed a kind of Messianic revelation.[2] Such was the famous propaganda of Tecumseh and his brother " the Prophet," who were men of noble character and

---

[1] Bishop Callaway, *Religious System of the Amazulu* (1870), p. 266: " There was a man named Unyadeni whose friends did not wish him to become an inyanga. They said, ' No; we do not wish so fine and powerful a man to become a mere thing which stays at home and does no work but merely divines.' So they laid his spirit. But there still remained in him signs which caused the people to say, ' If that man had been an inyanga, he would have been a very great man, an inyangisisa. "

[2] J. Mooney, *The Ghost Dance Religion*, Bureau of Ethnology, Washington, 1896.

high mentality, and in recent times we have the instances of the Ghost Dance Religion which led to the Sioux War of 1890, and the diffusion of the Peyote cult in the present century.

It is in North America that the cult of the visionary experience is most highly developed, since in many tribes it forms a regular part of the initiation of a tribesman, and here it is certainly not a mere hysterical crisis, but possesses a genuine religious and moral significance. Among the Iowa when a youth goes into solitude to prepare for his visionary experience, his father or teacher addresses him in the following words: "The time has come to use the charcoal (with which the neophyte smears his face). Let thy tears fall on our Mother, the Earth, that she may have pity on thee and help thee in thy need. Seek thy way; the Creator will help thee. He sends thee, perchance, a voice, and prophecies to thee, whether thou wilt gain renown in thy tribe or no. Perchance thou wilt dream of the Thunder or of some other being above, his helper or servant. May they vouchsafe thee long life! Entreat help of the Sun. The Sun is a great power. But if there comes some power out of the water or from the earth, take it not; let it be; turn not thy attention to it! Hear naught of it, otherwise thou wilt quickly die! For so must thou hold thyself. Be cautious. There are heavenly powers and powers of evil, and these seek to deceive thee. Thou must be ready to fast, for if Wakanda helps thee, thou wilt become a great man, a protector of thy people, and thou wilt obtain honour."[1]

[1] A. B. Skinner, in "Anthropological Papers of the American Museum of Natural History," XI, p. 739, etc. We may compare with this programme

The experience of an initiate during this ordeal often determined the whole course of a man's subsequent career. Francis Parkman records the case of a Dakota, the member of one of the most warlike families amongst a people of warriors, whose whole life was devoted to the cause of peace and to appeasing feuds and private quarrels, because the spirit of peace had appeared to him during his initiation under the form of an antelope, and had forbidden him to follow the path of war, like other men. And though this vocation ran contrary to the whole ethos of his tribe, it was accepted without question by his fellows on the strength of his supernatural revelation.

In addition, however, to the subjective experience of the vision which is the characteristic feature of this type of religion, Shamanism, whether of a debased or exalted form, also involves an element of training and traditional knowledge. The Shaman possesses a technique, a knowledge of magical rites and religious procedure, as well as a theory of the methods of healing, and some understanding of the properties of plants.

All this knowledge may be handed down from father to son in hereditary succession, or may be the professional tradition of an order. In central Australia, for example, while the medicine-man may owe his powers to the direct revelation of spirits, he may also undergo a training under an experienced elder, such as the *oknirabata*, or " great teacher," of the Arunta, who is also the chief authority in all matters connected

---

the experiences of an Australian medicine-man given by Howitt in his *Native Tribes of S.E. Australia;* that of the Siberian Shaman in Czaplica *Aboriginal Siberia*, pp.169; and the elaborate and strictly professional training of an Ashanti priest, who is also something of a Shaman, in Rattray *Religion and Art in Ashanti*, pp. 40-47. In all of them the visionary experience is of the first importance.

with the performance of the tribal rites and ceremonies. When this professional tradition of expert knowledge comes to outweigh in importance the element of personal experience, the technique of the medicine-man develops into a regular art or science, often of a very elaborate character. Sir James Frazer has pointed out what vast consequences this change involved for human progress. It meant that an order of men were set apart from their fellows, relieved from the necessity of labour, that they might devote themselves to the acquisition of knowledge. " It was at once their duty and their interest to know more than their fellows, to acquaint themselves with everything that could aid man in his arduous struggle with nature. The properties of drugs and minerals, the causes of rain and drought, of thunder and lightning, the changes of the seasons, the phases of the moon, the daily and yearly journeys of the Sun, the motions of the stars, the mystery of life, and the mystery of death. All these must have excited the wonder of these early philosophers, and stimulated them to find solutions of problems that were doubtless often thrust on their attention in the most practical form by the importunate demands of their clients, who expected them not merely to understand, but to regulate the great processes of nature for the good of man."[1]

Thus Sir James Frazer is completely justified in regarding magic as the first approach towards a systematic study of the external world, and the source of the earliest conception of an order of nature and of the existence of the law of causality. But while the magician is in a sense a kind of primitive scientist,

[1] Sir J. Frazer, *Lectures on the Early History of Kingship*, 1905, pp. 90-91.

he is at the same time a Shaman or a priest. It is impossible to agree with Frazer that magic is essentially non-religious and pre-religious—that "man essayed to bend nature to his wishes by the sheer force of spells and enchantments, before he strove to mollify a coy, capricious or irascible deity by the soft insinuation of prayer and sacrifice." On the contrary a developed system of magic is due to the elaboration and formalizing of a primitive type of religious experience—the ecstasy of the Shaman lies behind the stereotyped formulæ of the magician, just as the religious experience of a Buddha or a Mohammed lies behind the developed ritualism of modern Buddhism and Islam.

The vital change in primitive culture is not that from magic to religion, for, as we have seen, religion lies at the root of the whole development, but from Shamanism to Priesthood. When the latter stage is reached, man's relation to the supernatural powers that govern his existence is no longer dependent on the unregulated transports of the Shaman, but becomes a social function controlled by a regular order. As Wissler says, a Shaman may be a veritable idiot, but the priest must be a man of intellect,[1] and his influence brings a new principle of order into the whole life of primitive society.

Even the most anomalous and individualistic aspects of Shamanism acquire social significance when they are transferred to the hands of a priestly corporation. For example, the history of the Delphic oracle shows how the office of the diviner, when administered by an able priesthood, may become of transcendent social

[1] C. Wissler, *The American Indian*, p. 204.

importance for a whole civilization. Nor is this a unique phenomenon, for the Long Ju-Ju of Aro, the famous oracle of the Cross River, played a very similar part among the barbarous Ibo peoples of Southern Nigeria.[1]

But it is in the case of these functions which are pre-eminently social, i.e. the rites which deal with the physical welfare of the people and the safeguarding of their means of sustenance—that the socialization of religion has the most important results on the development of culture. As far back as palæolithic times, the evidence of the cave paintings suggests that one of the most important social functions was the attainment of success in hunting by magical practices which were intended to give man control over the beasts, which were the chief source of his food supply.[2] But it is probable that this hunting magic was associated with the individualistic type of Shamanism which is still found among the most backward peoples of North America, for example, the tribes of the Mackenzie basin, among whom the social unit is the small and unorganized band of hunters. A higher stage of organization is reached when a society becomes subdivided into a number of different groups, each of which has its own sacred rites, and is united by ceremonial or religious bonds. And just as the Shaman, or even the individual hunter, in a simpler phase of society has his own guardian spirit, usually in animal form, so now each group possesses a sacred bond with some particular

[1] In both cases the oracle was associated with a development of colonizing activity, and the priesthood of Aro Chuku was also a great commercial power in the land.
[2] See the chapter on " the Religion of the Hunter " in my *Age of the Gods* (Murray, 1928).

species of animal or plant. A number of different conceptions may enter into this totemic relationship. Indeed, the term totemism has been so loosely used that it is often made to cover all kinds of different ideas, from the belief in animal guardian spirits and the worship of animal gods, to the use of semi-heraldic tribal emblems.

The root of true totemism, however, seems to be found in the conception of the totem as a food giver, and in the rites for the conservation and increase of the means of subsistence. As among the hunting peoples of North America and Siberia, the buffalo and the bear are sacred animals, so in Australia every object which supplies the native with food, whether the wichetty grub, the grass seed, or the kangaroo, becomes the totem of a group. This aspect of totemism is seen most clearly in the ceremonies for the multi-plication of the totemic animal or plant, known among the Arunta as Intichiuma, for example, in the case of the wild grass totem. Here the magic rites have entirely lost their individualistic character. The head of the totem performs the rites which cause the growth of the wild grass seed, or the multiplication of the wild bees not for his own profit, since he is forbidden to partake of them except in a solemn ritual manner, but for the welfare of the people as a whole. He is in fact a true priest, a social functionary, who performs a sacrament, not for himself but for the community.

Moreover, in so far as these ceremonies take the form of a mimicry or imitation of the processes of nature, they afford an opportunity for men to acquire a knowl-edge and control over nature which is substantial and real, not merely an illusion of magical art. When, for example, the Australian native collects the grass seed and blows a little of it in all directions in order to make it grow plentifully, it is easy to see in the ceremony the germ of a development which might eventually lead to the discovery of agriculture. And in the same way when the Arctic peoples of Siberia rear a tame bear cub, " the common bear " as it is called, which is at last ceremonially killed in order to ensure a food supply of bear's meat for the year, we seem to be witnessing an early stage in the domestication of animals. It is true that the Australians have never attained to the agricultural stage, nevertheless, their peculiarly stereotyped culture seems to represent as it were a fossilized survival of a stage of culture intermediate between that of the mere food-gatherers and that of the primitive agriculturalists. The actual invention of agriculture may well have been a unique discovery which was diffused from a single centre of origin, but we have good reason to suppose that it arose in connection with a cult of natural fertility and as a result of the ritual imitation of the processes of nature.

One of the oldest and most universal forms of religion consists in the worship of the Mother Goddess, the goddess of the earth and of all that lives and grows. This divine figure appears all over the world in connection with the beginnings of the higher civilization in Mesopotamia and Syria, in the Ægean and Asia Minor, in prehistoric Europe, and even in West Africa and in the New World. The rude female figures, which represent idols of the goddess, or fertility charms, have been discovered by the spade of the archæologist in the earliest deposits of the prehistoric cultures, while in the higher civilizations the same figure reigns in the great temple cities of Babylonia and Asia Minor as she still does in modern India to-day.

And among many primitive peoples at the present day this deity is still worshipped, as we see in the following utterance recorded by K. T. Preuss, among the Kagaba Indians of French Guiana : " The mother of our songs, the mother of all our seed, bore us in the beginning of things, and she is the mother of all types of men, the mother of all nations. She is the mother of the Thunder, the mother of the streams, the mother of the trees and all things. She is the mother of the world and of the older brothers, the stone people. She is the mother of the fruits of the earth and of all things. She is the mother of our younger brothers, the French and the strangers. She is the mother of our dance paraphernalia, of all our temples, and she is the only mother we possess. She alone is the mother of the fire and the sun and the Milky Way. She is the mother of the rain, and the only mother we possess. And she has left us a token in all the temples—a token in the form of songs and dances."[1]

But the fertility cult finds its most characteristic expression in those symbolic representations of the divine marriage of the Great Mother, and of the death and resurrection of her divine child or lover, the god of vegetation, which formed the mysteries of so many ancient Asiatic cults, such as those of Ishtar and Tamnuz, of Attis and Cybele, and of Astarte and Adonis. And it is easy to see how the drama of the death and resurrection of the powers of nature would become

---

[1] K. T. Preuss, *Religion und Mythologie der Uitoto*, I, p. 169, in Radin op. cit., pp. 357-8.

inseparably bound up with symbolical representations such as the opening of the furrows, the sowing and watering of the seed, and the reaping of the sacred corn sheave. We may well believe that some such symbolic representation or imitation of the processes of nature may have actually given rise to a knowledge of agriculture, and that its practical utilization followed on its first performance as a sacred ritual art intended to promote the increase of the natural products of the soil. In the same way, the keeping of sacred animals, such as the bull and the cow, which were the symbols or the incarnations of the divine fecundity, may have led, in Western Asia, to the discovery of the art of the domestication and breeding of animals. For all these arts of husbandry were, to the men of the ancient world, no mere matters of practical economy, but sacred mysteries, the secret of which lay at the very heart of their religions.[1]

But whatever may be the final conclusions regarding the religious origins of agriculture and the domestication of animals, there can be no doubt that the earliest forms of the higher civilization were characterized by the development of the priesthood as an organized social order. The transition from Shamanism to priesthood approximately corresponds with the transition from the lower to the higher type of culture.

It is unfortunately impossible to study this process of evolution in the cultures of the old world, for the decisive step had already been taken before the beginnings of history. In America, however, where, as we

---

[1] The religous origins of agriculture and of the domestication of animals have been maintained by E. Hahn (*Die Entstehung der Pflugkultur* 1909), and recently by F. Wahle in the important article on *Wirtschaft* on Eberts' *Reallexikon der Vorgeschichte* vol. xiv. pp. 323–369.

have already said, the whole sequence of cultures is more recent than in Eurasia, it is still possible to find examples of very primitive types of agricultural societies, and even of the transitional phase between the culture of the hunter and that of the peasant. In every case there seems to be a very close association between the practice of agriculture and the development of ritual ceremonies and priestly organization. For while the diffusion of ritualism is wider than that of agriculture, its highest development is to be found in the early centres of agricultural civilization, and it steadily decreases in intensity as it radiates outwards from these centres.

The most remarkable of all these societies is that of the Pueblo Indians of Arizona and New Mexico, since, in spite of changes of population, their culture tradition has survived almost intact from prehistoric times; in fact it is essentially of the same type as the early neolithic peasant cultures of the Old World, especially the so-called Painted Pottery cultures, and it seems to carry us back to the first beginnings of the higher civilization such as underlie the earliest historic cultures of Sumer and Egypt. The whole life of the people centres in the rites concerned with the cultivation of the maize, and its fertilization by warmth and moisture. Dr. C. Wissler, the great authority on native American culture, writes: " The appearance of the clouds, the rain, maize planting, in fact the whole round of daily life is accompanied by ritualistic procedures, each group of priests performing its part at the appointed time. While essentially magical, these rituals contain a large amount of practical knowledge as to the care of seed and the time and place of planting, etc."[1] In spite of the comparatively small size of these communities, they possess a large number of different priesthoods and religious confraternities, each of which has its specific functions and ceremonials. Among the Hopi there are the snake priests, the priests of the sun and the calendar, the Horned Priests who perform the great annual ceremonies of the New Fire, and many more. And in all these ceremonies the corn maidens and the rude symbols which represent Alosaka, the power of germination, or Talatumsi, the earth mother, or " the elder sister of the dawn," play a leading part.[2]

Now when a ceremonial cycle of this type, based upon the agricultural year, has once been established, it is capable of being developed into a vast ritual order which embraces the whole social and intellectual life of society. This is what we find in the higher civilizations of Central America, such as those of the Maya and the Aztec peoples. In the case of the former, the development of the ritual cycle led to that amazing progress in astronomical and chronological science which is embodied in the great Maya calendar, with its ingenious system of interlocking cycles, and its simultaneous use of the Venus year of 584 days, as well as of the solar and lunar periods. This calendar is, as Wissler says, " not a dating device," but a ceremonial order which " provides the religious programme for each day in the year or a complete cycle of never ending services." The ritual order was at once the reflection and fulfilment of the cosmic order, since it co-ordinated the order of the heavens with that of the

---

[1] Wissler, *The American Indian*, p. 194-5, cf. 203.
[2] See the account of some of these Hopi ceremonies by Dr. Fewkes in Smithsonian Report, 1920, 1922, etc.

seasons, and by its ceaseless round of sacrifice and prayer assisted the powers of nature to function.

The same system was inherited by the later Aztec culture of Mexico which, however, in spite of its military power, stood on a far lower level of civilization than that of the old Maya city states. Mr. Spinden has aptly compared the relation between the two peoples to that between the Greek and Roman cultures, while the older Toltec culture of the Mexican highlands occupies the same relative position between the other two, as was held by the Etruscans in the ancient world.[1] Here the sacrificial aspect of ritual became of overwhelming importance, and expressed itself in a continual series of human sacrifices, usually accompanied by dramatic representations in which the victim impersonated the god. The fertility and rejuvenation of nature could only be secured by a copious expenditure of human blood, and the warlike character of the Aztec culture was due to the necessity of providing an annual supply of captives for the sacrificial rites.

Thus in both of these instances, as well as in the South American cultures, the civilization was essentially a development of the ritual order,[2] and when, as in the case of the Maya culture, the ritual was broken or its custodian, the priesthood, declined, the whole civilization fell into decay.

This ritual character of the archaic civilization is most clearly seen in the American cultures, for, as I have said, it is only in America that the early stages

[1] H. J. Spinden, *The Ancient Civilizations of Mexico and Central America*, p. 178-9.
[2] Thus even the game of ball, the ancestor of the modern basket ball, formed part of the ceremonial system, and the ball courts occupy an important place in the temple area.

of higher culture survived into historical times. Nevertheless there are plentiful traces of the existence of the same type of culture in the old World. Each of the archaic civilizations was a ritual civilization, and its character depended on the type of ritual that was predominant. Thus in ancient China the calendar seems to have possessed a ritual significance no less than among the Maya. The Emperor, the Son of Heaven, was the lord of the sacred calendar, and the whole state cultus was based on the idea of the ritual co-ordination of the social order with the cosmic order as manifested in the way of heaven. Even the sacred palace—the Ming T'ang—was arranged in accordance with this idea, as the House of the Calendar, and the Emperor moved from chamber to chamber according to the month of the year, changing his dress, his food, his ornaments, and even his music so as to harmonize with the changes of the seasons. In India, on the other hand, the emphasis of the ritual was placed on the sacrifice, and there the cosmic order was conceived as bound up with and actually dependent upon the sacrificial ritual.

In the case of India and China, however, we can only trace the vestiges of this early phase of civilization surviving under the forms of a higher type of culture. In Western Asia, on the other hand, we can follow the development of the archaic ritual civilizations back to a far earlier period, and see how the religion of the Mother Goddess presided over their origins. For the first development of the higher culture in the Near East, the beginnings of agriculture and irrigation and the rise of city life were profoundly religious in their conception. Men did not learn to control the forces of nature to make the earth fruitful, and to raise flocks and herds, as a practical task of economic organization in which they relied on their own enterprise and hard work. They viewed it rather as a religious rite by which they co-operated as priests and hierophants in the great cosmic mystery of the fertilization and growth of nature. The mystical drama, annually renewed, of the Mother Goddess, and her dying and reviving son and spouse was, at the same time, the economic cycle of ploughing, and seed time and harvest, by which the people lived. And the King was not so much the organizing ruler of a political community, as the priest and religious head of his people, who represented the god himself and stood between the goddess and her people, as the minister and inter-preter of the divine will.[1]

But it is only in highly conservative regions like Asia Minor that we can see this primitive religion in comparative simplicity. In Mesopotamia, at the very dawn of history in the 4th millenium B.C., it had already developed a highly specialized theology and temple ritual. The god and goddess of each city had acquired special characteristics and personalities, and had taken their place in a Sumerian pantheon. But Sumerian civilization still remained entirely religious in character. The god and the goddess were the acknowledged rulers of their city, the King was but their high priest and steward. The temple, the house of the god, was the centre of the life of the community, for the god was the chief landowner, trader and banker

[1] I have dealt with this subject at some length in *The Age of the Gods*, chs. v and vi.

and kept a great staff of servants and administrators. The whole city territory was, moreover, the territory of the god, and the Sumerians spoke not of the boundaries of the city of Kish or the city of Lagash, but of the boundaries of the god Enlil or the god Ningirshu. All that the king did for his city was undertaken at the command of the god and for the god. And the remains of the ancient literature that have come down to us prove that this is not merely the phraseology of the state religion, it represented a profound popular belief in the interdependence and communion of the city and its divinity.

In the case of Egypt also we find a no less intensely religious spirit impregnating the archaic culture. The Egyptian religion is, however, less homogeneous than that of Mesopotamia or of Asia Minor. In the first place, there is the worship of the animal gods of the nomes, which is the primitive religion of the natives of the Nile valley; secondly there is the cult of Osiris, which is essentially similar to that of the Asiatic nature god, Tammuz and Adonis, of whom we have just spoken, and which was perhaps introduced into the Delta in predynastic times from Syria or Palestine; finally there is the religion of the Sun god which became the official cult of the Pharaohs, and inspired the main development of the archaic Egyptian civilization.

Never perhaps before or since has a high civilization attained to the centralization and unification that characterized the Egyptian state in the age of the Pyramid Builders. It was more than state socialism, for it meant the entire absorption of the whole life of the individual in a cause outside himself. The whole vast bureaucratic and economic organization of the

Empire was directed to a single end, the glorification of the Sun god and his child the god King.

It is indeed one of the most remarkable spectacles in history to see all the resources of a great culture and a powerful state organized, not for war and conquest, not for the enrichment of a dominant class, but simply to provide the sepulchre and to endow the chantries and tomb-temples of the dead Kings. And yet it was this very concentration on death and the after life that gave Egyptian civilization its amazing stability. The Sun and the Nile, Re and Osiris, the Pyramid and the Mummy, as long as those remained, it seemed that Egypt must stand fast, her life bound up in the unending round of prayer and ritual observance. All the great development of Egyptian art and learning grew up in the service of this central religious idea, and when, in the age of final decadence, foreign powers took possession of the sacred kingdom, Libyans and Persians, Greeks and Romans all found it necessary to "take the gifts of Horus," and to disguise their upstart imperialism under the forms of the ancient solar theocracy, in order that the machinery of Egyptian civilization should continue to function.

VI

THE RISE OF THE WORLD RELIGIONS

IT is difficult to exaggerate the debt that the world owes to the archaic ritual cultures of the type described in the last chapter, for they laid the foundations on which the whole later development of civilization has been built. To them we owe the invention of writing and of the calendar, the discovery of the use of metals, architecture and engineering, and almost all the arts and crafts of daily life, as they are practised down to the present day in both the Near and the Far East. We can measure their achievement in some degree by their monuments—the pyramids and sun temples of Egypt, the canals and temple towers of Babylonia and the Maya and Toltec remains in America—which are unsurpassed in majesty of form and power of execution by the works of modern man in spite of his vastly increased control over matter.

But while they realized an enormous material progress—relatively the greatest perhaps that the world has ever seen—this progress was strictly limited. Each culture was bound up with an absolutely fixed ritual form from which it could not be separated. When once it had realized its potentialities, and embodied its ritual order in a complete social and material form, it became stationary and unprogressive.

We see the consequences of this in the great civilizations of the Near East which were not permanently affected by barbarian invasions. The very features of the Egyptian culture which we have noted as evidence of its strength and permanence are also the measure of its limitations. From the point of view of material civilization, the Egyptians were the equals or even the superiors of the Greeks and Romans who had conquered them. But it was an entirely conservative civilization, bound up with the religious forms of the distant past. Even her conquerors had to fall in with these forms, in order to rule the country. The old temple services still went on, the old sacred state still subsisted. Only Ptolemy or Cæsar had stepped into the shoes of the Pharaoh. Nothing is more curious than to see, on the wall of the later Egyptian temples, the figures of Tiberius or Ptolemy, depicted in Egyptian dress with the high white crown of the Pharaohs on their heads, in the act of adoring Isis and Osiris or the crocodile-headed god Sebek, and to read their European names followed by the old divine titles, " Son of the Sun, lord of both lands, beloved of Ptah and Isis." The whole of Egypt had become a great archæological museum, and if her culture survived, it was like the survival of a mummy, not that of a living being.

The same process would no doubt have occurred in the case of the other ancient civilizations, had they been allowed to follow their own line of development without external interference. In the majority of cases, however, the tradition of the archaic culture did not survive intact.

From the third millennium B.C. onwards, the societies of the higher culture were exposed to a series of invasions of more warlike but less civilized peoples, such as the peoples of Indo-European stock, which gradually led to the formation of new nations and cultures. The invaders, however, brought no impulse towards a higher material civilization. They came as destroyers rather than creators, like the barbarians who conquered the Roman Empire, or the Turkish invaders of the Near East. And, as in these cases, they owed their progress in civilization almost entirely to the elements of culture that they took over from the conquered peoples.

Nevertheless in the first millennium B.C. a cultural change of the most profound significance passed over the world, a change that was not confined to any one people or culture, but which made itself felt almost simultaneously from India to the Mediterranean and from China to Persia. It was, however, a change of thought rather than a revolution of material culture. It was due to the first appearance of new spiritual forces which have been active in the world ever since and which still influence the minds of men to-day. The teachings of the Hebrew prophets and the Greek philosophers, of Buddha and the authors of the Upanishads, of Confucius and Lao Tzu, are not the half-comprehended relics of a vanished world, like the religious literature of Egypt and Babylonia; they are of perennial significance and value. They have the same importance in the intellectual and spiritual life of mankind that the material achievements of the Archaic

Civilization possess in the sphere of material culture. Like the latter, they have laid a permanent foundation on which all later ages have built, and on which our own intellectual and religious tradition is based.

So great is the originality and power of the age which saw the rise of the world religions that it is easy to underestimate its own debt to the past. What link can there be between the Hellenic vision of an intelligible universe or the ethical humanism of Confucius and the bloody rites and barbarous myths of the old pagan culture?

Nevertheless, just as the culture of the new peoples was based on the tradition of the Archaic Civilization that they had conquered, so also they had inherited much of the intellectual and religious conceptions of the older world. But the dual character of the new cultures tended to produce a spirit of criticism and reflection which had been absent in the earlier stage of civilization. Men could no longer accept the existing state of society and human life as a manifestation of the divine powers. The destruction of the old theocratic order had left its mark on the popular consciousness, and everywhere we find a tendency to idealize the memory of the vanished order as a golden age when the gods had ruled mankind before the coming of injustice and strife. In contrast to this idealization of the past, the present appeared as an age in which the divine order was no longer observed, and evil and wrongdoing ruled supreme. And thus there arose a sense of moral dualism, an opposition between that which is and that which ought to be, between the way of man and the way of the gods. Men compared the world they knew with an ideal social and moral order and passed judgment upon it accordingly.

In this way, the central belief that underlies the archaic culture—the conception of a sacred order which governs alike the way of nature and the life of man—continued to exercise a vital influence on the mind of the new age, but it was at the same time remoulded and transformed. The idea which the previous age had expressed in a ritual form became moralized and spiritualized. The sacred order was no longer a ceremonial system, but a moral law of justice and truth.

Thus the ancient conception of a sacred ritual order was everywhere the starting point from which the new religious development proceeded. The connection is to be seen most clearly, perhaps, in the case of China, where the older type of culture had survived with less breach of continuity than elsewhere. Here the new moral teaching of Confucius was essentially connected with the old idea of a ritual order. Its importance in his eyes consisted not in the ethical ideals themselves, but in their application to the traditional rites. Indeed the Rites have the same importance for Confucianism that the Law possesses for Judaism.

They are not, as the Western observer is apt to suppose, a matter of social etiquette; they are nothing less than the external manifestation of that eternal order that governs the universe, which is known as the Tao, the Way of Heaven.

" They have their origin in Heaven," says the Book of the Rites, " and the movement of them reaches to earth. The distribution of them extends to all the business of life. They change with the seasons: they agree in reference to the variations of lot and condition. In regard to man they serve to nurture his nature." (Li-Ki, VII.)[1]

On one occasion Yen-Yen asked Confucius whether the Rites were really of such urgent importance. He answered : "It was by these rules that the ancient Kings sought to represent the ways of Heaven and to regulate the feelings of men. Therefore he who neglects or violates them may be spoken of as dead, and he who observes them as alive." . . . "Therefore these rules are rooted in Heaven, have their correspondencies on Earth, and are applicable to spiritual beings." (Lu-Yun, IV, 5 and I, 4).

The true greatness and originality of Confucius consists in his having given this ritual order an ethical content. Instead of regarding the rites as magically efficacious or being satisfied with an exterior standard of obedience to them, he demanded the interior adhesion of the whole man. The word Li which plays so important a part in the Confucian teaching, and which is commonly translated " Propriety," really signifies, not an external correctness of behaviour, but the conformity of the individual to the order which governs not only the life of society but the whole course of nature. The " Superior Man" must conform himself to the Tao not only in his outward conduct, but in his mind and his will. Thus the great Confucian virtue of benevolence or altruism (Jen) is not an emotional love of others, it is the renunciation of self-interest and egotism, and the merging of self in the universal order. So, too, the virtue of Justice (Yi) which consisted originally in the strict observance

[1] Trans. J. Legge (Sacred Books of the East vol. III).

of class distinctions and the exact apportionment of social rights—was transformed by Confucianism into an ideal of moral rectitude and justice.

Moreover, this moral self-culture is not limited in its effects to the inner life of the individual. It radiates downwards from the King or the Sage upon all his subjects and disciples; it becomes the link which binds Heaven and Earth, Man and Nature, together in a cosmic harmony which is the supreme ideal of Confucianism.[1] " When the Son of Heaven moves in his virtue like a chariot, with music as his driver, while all the Princes conduct their mutual intercourse according to the Rites, the Great Officers maintain the order between them according to the laws, inferior officers complete one another by their good faith, and the common people guard one another in a spirit of harmony, all under the sky is in good condition. This produces the state that is called the Great Unity." (Li—Ki. XVII.) Thus the old ritual order of the archaic culture became in the hands of the Confucians the basis of an ethical interpretation of life which has been the ruling conception of Chinese civilization ever since.

Now the same conception of a universal order is also of fundamental importance in the religious development of India and Persia. It appears in the Rigveda, the most ancient of the sacred books of India, under the name of Rta or Rita—the same word which is found in Old Persian as Arta, and as Asha in the Zend-Avesta. It is usually translated as Order or Right, but it is difficult to find any equivalent for it in

---

[1] " The Superior Man brings Heaven and Earth into Order; the Superior Man forms a triad with Heaven and Earth; he is the controller of all things, the father and mother of the people." Hsüntze Book IX, 11, trans. H. Dubs.

123

modern English since it is at once cosmic, ritual and moral. It is seen primarily in the ordered course of nature, the succession of the seasons and the movement of the heavens. The year is the wheel of Rita, the wheel with twelve spokes. The sun is " the clear and visible face of Rita," and the rivers follow the sacred Rita in their unceasing flow. But its ethical aspect is even more important. It is usually associated in the Rigveda with Varuna, the righteous god who watches over justice and punishes sin. He is " the foundation of Rita," " the guardian of Holy Rita," and the just man prays that he may help " to increase Varuna's spring of Rita," an expression which is almost identical with that used in the Avesta which speaks of " swelling the spring of Asha." Finally, Rita, like the Latin *ritus*, is pre-eminently applied to the ritual order of the sacrifice. The sacrificial fire is " the shoot of Rita, born in the Rita," and it carries the offerings to the gods by way of Rita.

This aspect of the conception, though it is the most primitive of all, was destined to have the greatest influence on the religious development of India. In the Brahmanas a regular philosophy of ritual was worked out, according to which the order of the sacrifice is the efficient cause of the order of nature, and the Brahman, the sacred sacrificial formula, is conceived as the ultimate force behind the universe. In Persia, on the other hand, the course of development was in the opposite direction. There, too, Asha was no doubt originally a ritual conception, and it retained its close connection with the sacred fire until the end. But it was the moral aspect that was most emphasized. Asha becomes the personification of the divine righteousness. It finds its expression in moral purity and truth, and the servants of Asha are they who "cause the world to advance" by husbandry and good works.

The existence of a similar conception in the Greek world is, perhaps, not so clearly evident. The tradition of the archaic culture survived in Greece in a more sporadic and irregular way than elsewhere. It was not embodied in an organized priesthood, as in India, or in a fixed political order as in China. Nevertheless, in spite of this lack of cultural continuity, the ritual tradition of the archaic culture continued to rule men's lives. The new mythology of the Olympian deities was of far less importance to the religious man than the due performance of the sacred rites whose origins were deeply rooted in the archaic past. The theology of the Greeks was a thing of yesterday, as Herodotus remarks, but their religious practices were of immemorial antiquity. Men might believe what they would concerning the nature of the gods so long as they maintained an exact and scrupulous performance of the Rites, for that alone could ensure the safety of the city and the fertility of the soil. The law of sacrifice was "the ancient and best law"—νόμος δ'ἀρχαῖος ἄριστος—on which the whole social order rested.

But this ceremonial tradition was also bound up with ethical conceptions. The ideas of moral and ritual purity were inseparable from one another, and both of them were regarded as a human participation in the universal law of Dike—Eternal Right. This is the principle in Hellenic thought which corresponds most closely to the Rita and Asha of the East Aryan

125

peoples.[1] Like the latter, it finds its expression in the whole cosmic order, and both Homer and Hesiod regard an act of human injustice as involving a disturbance of the course of nature. " When men follow justice," writes Hesiod, " the whole city blooms, the earth bears rich harvests, and children and flocks increase, but to the unjust all nature is hostile, the people waste away from famine and pestilence, and a single man's sin may bring ruin on a whole city."[2]

But this conception of a universal order which governs the whole course of nature finds its fullest expression in Greek philosophy. Both Pythagoras and Heraclitus regarded the principle of measure and order as the underlying cause of all things. " Even the Sun," says Heraclitus " cannot exceed his measures, for if he does so, the Erinyes, the handmaids of Dike, will find him out." Nor is this principle limited to the material and physical. It is " the one divine law by which all human laws are fed," it is the Way of God, " the thought by which all things are steered through all things."[3] The same idea finds its classical expression in Plato, above all in *The Laws* which are based no less than the teaching of Confucius upon the idea that the law of social life must be a reflection of and a participation in the universal divine order which rules the universe, and which is manifested primarily in the order of the stars.[4]

Thus in all the great civilization, from China to

---

[1] See on this point F. M. Cornford, *From Religion to Philosophy*, 1912, p. 172-7.
[2] Hesiod, *Works and Days*, 217-277. Cf. also the passage in Euripedes *Medea*, 410, " the springs of the holy rivers flow backwards, and Dike and all things are turned upside down."
[3] Heraclitus frs. 29, 91, 96, 19 tr. Burnet, *Early Greek Philosophy*, 2nd ed.
[4] Cf. esp *Laws*, 716 and *Epinomis* 986 c. " that universal order which Law the most divine of all things has marshalled in visible array."

the Ægean, the beginning of the new movement of thought is marked by the appearance of the conception of a universal order which is both spiritual and material, at once the order of justice and the order of nature. But the intellectual revolution did not stop short at this point; on the contrary it was but the stepping stone to a further development. The pioneers of thought did not rest content with the conception of an order immanent in the world, which manifests itself in the course of nature and the moral life of man. They sought for a yet higher principle, an absolute reality which transcends the order of nature and all limited forms of existence.

This search for the Absolute found its earliest and most complete expression in India, where it developed, not as might have been expected from the comparatively advanced ethical ideas connected with the worship of Varuna, but from the more primitive type of religion which is represented by the ritual magic of the Brahmanas and which perhaps owes its origin to the native tradition of the conquered Dravidian culture.

But it has its roots in an even older and more universal stage of thought than that of the Archaic Culture, for it is derived from that vague and obscure intuition of transcendent being which is, as we have seen, the ultimate basis of primitive religion. Like the Orenda and the Wakan of the North American Indians, the word Brahman signifies at once the priestly formula or spell, and a self-existent principle or essence which is the ultimate force in the universe.

The progress of Indian thought from the religion of the Brahmanas to the religion of the Upanishads, consists in the conversion of this primitive idea of

Brahman as a kind of magical potency or " Zauber-fluidum " into an absolute metaphysical principle. The first step in the development took place when men transferred the value of the rites from their external performance to their esoteric significance. The idea of Brahman was abstracted from the sacrifice which became merely a symbolic representation of the higher reality. At first this reality was conceived cosmologically as the world essence or universal substance: Brahman was identified with space or with Prana, the breath of life. But these cosmological explanations did not satisfy the quest for reality which inspired the thinkers of the Upanishads. They sought not merely to get beyond the mythology and the external ritual of religious tradition, but to pass beyond the outward appearance of things, beyond the created universe, so as to reach the one absolute being which alone is true, which alone *is*.

Now the great achievement of the thinkers of the Upanishads, the discovery which has dominated Indian religion and thought ever since, was the identification of this supreme principle with the Atman or Self. This Self or soul is the ground of everything that exists, it is " the web on which the world is woven." Above all, it is the ground of our own consciousness, the soul of our souls, for the human self and the ultimate Self are in a sense identical.

" He who, dwelling in the earth, is other than the earth, whom the earth knows not, whose body the earth is, who inwardly rules the earth, is thyself, the Inward Ruler, the Deathless."

" He who, dwelling in the mind, is other than the mind whom the mind knows not, whose body the mind is, who inwardly rules the mind, is thyself, the Inward Ruler, the Deathless."

" He unseen sees, unheard hears, unthought thinks, uncomprehended comprehends. There is no other than he who sees. There is no other than he who hears, there is no other than he who thinks, there is no other than he who comprehends. He is thyself, the Inward Ruler, the Deathless."[1]

Thus the supreme principle is no longer identified with the world substance or even with the cosmic process, as in the naïve pantheism of the Brahmanas. It is essentially a spiritual reality, which transcends all finite modes of being. It can be described only by negatives, " Neti, neti, not thus, not thus," for " the Atman is silence." " When the sun has set and the moon has gone down and the fire is quenched and speech is hushed," the light of the Atman shines forth.

And with the realization of this principle of transcendence, the whole spiritual attitude of Indian religion became transformed.

The knowledge of Brahman was sought not, as in the earlier period, for the power that it conferred over nature, and the material rewards of long life, wealth and prosperity, but for its own sake as the supreme good. All the good works of the old religion—the worship of the gods, sacrifice, and the knowledge of the rites—have lost their value. They can only procure relative goods—prosperity in this world and a happy after life. True happiness is to be found only in the realization of the unity of the Atman—the supreme unification of the soul with the Absolute, which alone can free man from the penalty of rebirth.

[1] *Brihad-aranyaka Upanishad*, III, vii, tr. L. D. Barnett,

" As is a man's desire, so is his will, and as is his will so is his deed, and whatever deed (Karma) he does that will he reap."

" When all the desires that once entered his heart are undone, then does the mortal become immortal, then he obtains Brahman. And as the slough of a snake lies on an anthill dead and cast away, thus lies his body; but that disembodied immortal spirit is Brahman only, is only light."[1]

Thus the conception of a transcendent reality became the foundation of a new moral ideal which no longer had any relation to social rights and duties. It was an ethic of absolute renunciation and detachment —the flight of the Alone to the Alone. " Knowing Brahman a man becomes a saint; hermits wander forth seeking Him for their world. Understanding this the ancients desired not offspring, ' what is offspring to us who have this Self for our world.' So having departed from desire of sons, from desire of substance and desire of the world, they went about begging."[2]

How far removed is this attitude from the simple acceptance of the good things of life that is shown in the nature religions and in the archaic culture that is founded upon them !

The one end of life, the one task for the wise man, is Deliverance; to cross the bridge, to pass the ford from death to Life, from appearance to Reality, from time to Eternity—all the goods of human life in the family or the state are vanity in comparison with this. And so there arose in ancient India a whole series of

[1] *Brihad-aryanaka Upanishad*, IV, iv, tr. Max Müller.
[2] Op. cit. IV, iv, 22.

different schools of thought, each of which attempted to find the way of deliverance by means of some special discipline of salvation. The way of deliverance by the knowledge of the Atman is the classical example of these systems, and it has remained the basis of orthodox Indian thought ever since. Nevertheless, it does not stand alone; even in the Upanishads themselves it co-exists with other elements which were destined to become the bases of independent systems of thought. There was the old ritual doctrine of salvation by works which remained the normal belief of orthodox Brahmanic society, there were the cosmological theories which admitted the reality of matter and the elements, and which ultimately issued in the Sankhya philosophy, and finally there was the way of deliverance through asceticism whether physical austerities and penance (tapas) or by mental concentration and self discipline (yoga).

This is the most important element of all, since it underlies the whole religious development from the age of the Rigveda[1] down to the rise of the great monastic orders of the Jains and the Buddhists. But the ascetic ideal underwent a gradual change under the influence of the new movement of thought. The figure of the Muni or Shaman who acquires magical powers by self-torture and physical austerities gives place to that of the monk who seeks salvation by meditation and self discipline, in the same way that the conception of Brahman became transformed from a magical spell into a transcendent spiritual principle.

It was in Buddhism that the ascetic ideal found its highest expression, and Buddhism is also the most

[1] Cf. *Rigveda*, X, 136, which describes the Sun as the Great Ascetic.

complete and thorough-going example of the new disciplines of salvation. The thinkers of the Upanishads were primarily interested in their speculations concerning Brahman and the true nature of being, deliverance was a secondary question. To the Buddhist, on the other hand, the problem of deliverance was the one vital issue. " One thing only do I teach, O Monks," said the Buddha, " sorrow and the ending of sorrow." " As the sea has everywhere one taste, the taste of salt, so my teaching has one flavour, the flavour of Deliverance."

The Buddha expressly condemned all attempts to enquire into or to define the nature of this supreme goal. Salvation was to be found not in metaphysical knowledge, but in the strenuous moral endeavour which destroys desire, the root of all suffering and of physical existence itself.

Thus Buddhism arose as a movement of reaction to the intellectualism of the Upanishads and the philosophical schools. It reasserted the moral element of the conception of Rita—order—which had been subordinated to its ritual and cosmological aspects ever since the days of the Rigveda. It stands in the same opposition to the Upanishads, as Confucianism did to Taoism—as a moral discipline against a mystical cosmology and a metaphysical doctrine of Being. Like Confucianism, it claimed to be the " doctrine of the Mean," which alone can afford a true form of behaviour for the guidance of the sage. It is, indeed, more exclusively ethical in its content than Confucianism itself, since its moral teaching was not engrafted on the old ritual tradition. The moral law—the Dharma—existed in itself and by itself as the one principle of order and intelligibility in an illusory universe. For the cosmic order itself, as seen in the external course of nature, has no reality —" the wheel of existence is empty with a twelve-fold emptiness." Behind the appearance of things there is no transcendent reality, as the Upanishads taught, neither Brahman nor the Atman. There is only the " sorrowful wheel " of existence driven round by ignorance and lust, and the path of moral deliverance, the *via negativa* of the extinction of desire which leads to Nirvana—the eternal beatific silence.

" In the mind of him who realizes the insecurity of this transient life arises the thought : All on fire is this ceaseless flux, a blazing flame ! Full of despair it is and very fearful ! Oh that I might reach a state where Becoming is at an end ! How calm, how sweet would be that end of all defects, of all craving and passion—that great Peace—this Nirvana ! " " Is there any place where a man may stand, and, ordering his life aright, realize Nirvana ? " " Yes, O King, Virtue is that place."[1]

Thus in Buddhism the ethical tendencies of the new movement of thought attained their extreme development. The absolute supremacy of the moral law was secured, and the whole of existence was reduced to purely spiritual and ethical terms. But this moral absolutism involved the denial of all other aspects of reality. The supreme affirmation of the moral will was an act of self-destruction which denied nature and even life itself.

It was only in India that this extreme stage of nihilism was reached, in which the very existence of the human

[1] From the *Milinda Pañha*, The Questions of King Menander.

soul and of the Absolute itself was abolished, but elsewhere we find the same tendency to turn away from human life and the external order of the world in search of a transcendent principle. Even in China, the ethical positivism of Confucius did not reign unchallenged. Just as in India the principle of the ritual order—the Brahman—was transformed by the writers of the Upanishads into the metaphysical concept of pure being, so, too, in China there existed a school which interpreted the Tao, the universal order of the archaic culture, not like the Confucians as the principle of moral and social order, but in a mystical and transcendental sense. They believed that there existed behind the visible ever changing movement of the universe, a higher spiritual principle, which, itself unchanging, is the source of change; itself beyond existence, is the source of all that exists. Lao Tzu writes: " There is something undefined and yet complete which precedes the birth of Heaven and Earth. O Immovable! O Formless! which alone is without changing, which penetrates all things with alteration. It may be called the Mother of the Universe."[1] And Chuang Tzu, the greatest of the later Taoists who flourished in the 4th century B.C. writes in the same strain. " O my master, my master! Thou who destroyest all things without being cruel, Thou who doest good to ten thousand generations without being kind, Thou who wert before the ages and who art not old, Thou coverest the heavens, Thou bearest up the Earth, Thou art the effortless creator of all forms. To know thee thus, is the supreme joy."[2]

[1] Lao Tzu, ch. XXV, A, ed., and tr. Wieger, *Les Pères du Système Taoïste*.
[2] Chuang Tzu, ch. XIII, A, ed. Wieger. Op. cit.

134

Consequently the ethical ideal of the Taoists was one of quietism and spiritual detachment. They despised the traditional learning of the Confucian scholars as " the dregs and leavings of the ancients." The true knowledge is to be found neither in tradition nor in discursive reasoning, but in the mystical contemplation which leads to the direct intuition of reality. The wise man will take no part in the life of the state or in the business of human affairs, he will live in solitude as a hermit, conforming his spirit to the universal Tao whose influence is felt in the desert and the mountains, not in the ways of men.

It is obvious that such beliefs can afford no basis for social activity and no incentive to material progress, though they may bear rich fruit in literature and art. The whole tendency of the new movement of thought as represented by Buddhism and the religion of the Upanishads as well as by the Taoist mysticism, is to cause a turning away from human life and social activity towards the Absolute.

Even the higher *rational* activity of the philosopher and the scientist loses all its value and significance in the presence of the all-absorbing unity of pure Being.

This is stated with exceptional fullness and precision in a remarkable Taoist treatise of the T'ang period (8th century A.D.)—the Kwan-Yinn-Tzu. It is probably influenced by Buddhist philosophical ideas, but this is of little importance, since the Buddhist and Taoist standpoints in these matters are almost indistinguishable.

" Outside the Principle, the Tao, all is nothing. Everything that seems to exist forms part of the unity of the Tao. In this absolute and universal unity, there is no succession, no time, no distances. In the Tao a day and a hundred years, a furlong and a hundred leagues do not differ. . . . We must not, therefore, speak of laws of nature and of supposed breaches of these laws, such as changes of form or of sex, levitation, fire that does not burn and water that does not drown, monsters, prodigies and so forth. There is no such thing as a prediction, since time does not exist, and consequently there is no future. There is no such thing as levitation, since there is no space. The Tao is Unity which is contained in a single point, and has no past or future. I am one with all beings, and all beings are one with the Tao. Every phenomenon results from the play of the Tao, not from law. For a corpse to rise and walk, for a man to catch fish in a basin, or to come in and go out through a door that is painted on the wall is no anomaly, since there is no rule." "To distinguish between cause and effect, agent and product is illusion and fiction. The common herd imagine that noise is produced by a drum, when it is beaten by a man with a drumstick. But in reality, there is neither drum nor drumstick nor drummer. Or rather Drum-drumstick-drummer are the Tao which has produced in itself the phenomenon of drumming. The words signify nothing, seeing that the things signified do not exist."

"That which is seen in a state of waking is no more real than that which is seen in dreams. And the man who sees is no more real than that which he sees. The man who dreams and the man of whom he dreams are no more real the one than the other."

136

"It is because he knows that nobody exists, that the Sage is equally benevolent and indifferent to everybody."[1]

And a similar idea finds classical expression in the verses of Kien-Wenn, the Chinese emperor of the 6th century A.D.—who wrote:

> Do I sleep? Do I wake?
> Does that which I love exist?
> Are not all things the imagination of the Universal
>   Soul?
> Am not I myself part of the great Seer
> Of the Great Dreamer, who in the long night
> Dreams the great cosmic dream."[2]

This denial of the reality of the world of phenomena and even of the principle of causality is still more characteristic of Indian thought. Both the doctors of later Mahayana Buddhism, such as Nagarjuna or Asangha, and those of the later Vedanta, such as Sankara, teach that only the One exists, and that the appearance of the manifold is mere illusion, the work of Maya. The material universe is, in fact, a kind of cosmic nightmare—an illusory elephant, Mayahasti, so Gaudapada terms it. The only true reality is to be found in the intuition of the Absolute which the ascetic attains in trance and ecstasy.

In fact the religion of the new age marks in some respects a return to the individualism and the concentration on the personal experience of vision and ecstasy which characterizes the primitive Shaman.

[1] Kwan-Yinn Tzu, tr. Wieger, *Histoire des croyances religieuses et des opinions philosophiques en Chine*, 2nd ed., 1922, pp. 570-573.
[2] Tr. Wieger *La Chine à travers les âges* p. 166.

The material civilization of the oriental world owed its preservation mainly to the continued survival of the tradition of the archaic culture. In China the latter was consecrated and preserved in a somewhat rationalized form by the influence of Confucian orthodoxy. In India, on the other hand, the absolute metaphysical view of life was theoretically triumphant, and ruled the whole civilization. Nevertheless even there the old type of culture and the cult of the powers of nature with which it was associated continued to subsist with but little change. The ancient myths and rites are interpreted as the symbols of a higher reality by the followers of the new religious philosophy, while to the common people they retain their old meaning and continue to embody the mysterious forces of the physical world that rule the peasants' life. Indeed, in the course of time they tend to re-absorb the higher forms of religion that had seemed to replace them. Not only the worship of the Mother Goddess, and the archaic temple cultus, but thoroughly primitive forms of animism and magic gradually force their way into the bosom of the higher religions themselves. This is most strikingly evident in North-east India and in Thibet. Here Buddhism itself became contaminated by Shamanism and magic, and, by a strange paradox, the most abstract ethical system that the world has ever known gave birth to the monstrous deities and obscene rites of the Tantras.

Thus the oriental cultures that are based upon the new type of religion tend to become stationary or retrograde. They do not advance in power and knowledge, or in control over their material environment. By degrees the older type of culture from which they have arisen reasserts its power and absorbs them, in the same way that the jungle swallows up the ruined splendour of Ankhor and Anuradhapura.

It is true that the Indian development shows the tendencies of the new movement of thought in their most extreme and uncompromising form. In the West, at least, the intellectual revolution of the 6th to the 4th centuries B.C. does not seem in any way inconsistent with material progress; indeed that age witnessed a remarkable advance of civilization in every direction. At first sight nothing could seem farther removed from the oriental spirit of asceticism and world refusal than the Hellenic view of the world, with its frank acceptance of life and its boundless curiosity and intellectual freedom. Nevertheless, it is easy to exaggerate the contrast. In point of fact we find the same spiritual forces at work in the Hellenic world as in India and the Far East. Even the Indian doctrines of transmigration and release find their counterpart in the West in the Orphic and Pythagorean teachings. What could be more Indian in spirit than the Orphic discipline of salvation by which the purified soul attains to release from " the sorrowful wheel " of continued reincarnation?

In the same way Empedocles regarded human life as the penalty of former sin, and sought, like a Jain ascetic, to obtain release by the scrupulous avoidance of injury to any living creature. He taught that the many-coloured world of appearances owed its very existence to the principle of " accursed strife " which had clouded and defiled the pure white light of true being, so that reality was no longer as it had been in the beginning and as it would be in the end, " a perfect sphere, equal in every side and without limit, rejoicing in its circular solitude." (frs. 27 and 28).

Thus in Greece, no less than in India and China, the realization of the unity of the cosmic order inevitably led to the recognition of a higher reality which transcends all change and limitation. As the writers of the Upanishads had developed the conception of Brahman from a quasi-physical world-substance into the absolute Atman or Self, so, too, in Greece the physical unity of the old Ionian thinkers was gradually replaced by the metaphysical principle of pure Being. It was in the philosophy of Plato that this theory of a transcendent reality attained its classical expression in the West. The vision of Eternity that had so long absorbed the mind of the East, at last burst on the Greek world with dazzling power. With Plato, the Western mind turns away from the many-coloured changing world of experience to that other world of the eternal Forms, " where abides the very Being with which true knowledge is concerned, the colourless, formless, intangible essence, visible only to the mind, the pilot of the soul "[1] ; " a nature which is everlasting, not growing or decaying, or waxing or waning, but Beauty only, absolute, separate, simple and everlasting which without diminution and without increase is imparted to the ever-growing and perishing beauties of all other things."[2]

Such a view of the world seems to involve an ethic of renunciation and detachment like that of the Indian ascetic. For " if man had eyes to see Divine Beauty, pure and clear and unalloyed, not clogged with the pollutions of mortality and all the colours and vanities

[1] *Phaedrus*, 247.   [2] *Symposium*, 211.

of human life,"[1] all earthly things must lose their savour. His one aim will be " to fly away from earth to heaven," to recover the divine and deific vision which once " we beheld, shining in pure light, pure ourselves and not yet enshrined in the living tomb which we carry about with us now that we are imprisoned in the body, like the oyster in its shell."[2]

Nevertheless the Platonic mysticism differs from that of the oriental religions in that it is essentially a mysticism of the intelligence which seeks illumination not so much by asceticism and ecstasy as by the discipline of scientific knowledge. The Platonic ideal has been well defined by an ancient writer as " to seek after the mysterious Good and to be happy by geometry." For the object of the higher sciences was not in the view of Plato—or indeed of the Greek world in general—a utilitarian one. Geometry is " no mere human marvel but a miracle of God's invention,"[3] and the study of it leads the mind away from the corruptible and perishing to the contemplation of true being and eternal order.[4] To the man who follows this path there will be revealed a common bond binding together every geometrical diagram, every related group of numbers, every combination of the musical scale, and the single related movement of the revolutions of all the heavenly bodies into a single intelligible harmony,[5] and so he will be brought to the shore of that vast sea of beauty where the transcendent reality of the absolute beauty is at last revealed to him.[6]

But this vision of the world *sub specie aeternitatis* tended hardly less than the Indian doctrine of the illusory

---

[1] *Symposium*, 211. [3] *Epinomis*, 990 D. [5] *Epinomis*, 991 E.
[2] *Phaedrus*, 250. [4] *Republic*, 526 etc. [6] *Symposium*, 210.

nature of the universe to turn away men's minds from the world of common experience. It became impossible to attach any ultimate importance to the changes of the temporal process. For though the earth was not itself eternal, it was modelled on an eternal pattern, and time itself " imitates eternity, and moves in a circle measured by number." And since the perfect motion of the heavenly spheres is always circular, the process of temporal change must be circular also. It is not only plants and animals that go through a cycle of growth and decay. All created things have their appointed numbers and revolutions, and the cycle of the world and of time itself is fulfilled in the perfect year, when the heavens have performed a complete revolution and the planets find themselves in the same relation to one another that they were at the beginning. Then the cosmic process begins anew and all things recur in their former order.

This theory of the Great Year and the recurrent cycle of cosmic change is closely bound up with the astral theology which is expounded in the Epinomis. It is not, however, peculiar to Plato, since it had already made its appearance in the Greek world as early as the days of Heraclitus. Indeed, it was common to all the great civilizations of the ancient world, and its influence extended from Syria and Mesopotamia to Persia and India and China, where it has retained its importance down to the present day.[1] It is probable that the whole system had its origin in Meso-

---

[1] The system has attained its most elaborate development in China. The Chinese Great Year consists of twelve months or " Confluences," each of which is as long as the Great Year which the Greeks ascribed to Heraclitus, i.e. 10800 years. We have now reached the year 68943 of the whole cycle, and in the following Great Month, the period of the decline of Heaven and Earth will begin.

potamia where astronomy and the astral theology with which it was associated had attained a high pitch of development during the Neo-Babylonian Period (605–538) and that it was gradually diffused from this centre in all directions. It was, however, only among the Greeks that it passed from the sphere of magic and astrology to that of science and philosophy, and became part of a rational interpretation of the universe. Owing to the influence of Plato and the early Academy, it passed into the common intellectual tradition of the Hellenic world. Even Aristotle, in spite of his revolt against the Platonic idealism and his realization of the importance of sensible experience, was profoundly influenced by this view of the world. To him, also, the highest knowledge was to be found in the contemplation of the universe as a manifestation of perfect and unchanging Being. All progress is but a part of the process of generation and corruption, which is confined to the sublunary world—" the hollow of the Moon "—and which depends on the local movements of the heavenly spheres.

All such change must necessarily be cyclic. " For if," he says, " the movement of heaven appears periodic and eternal, then it is necessary that the details of this movement and all the effects produced by it will also be periodic and eternal."[1] Nor is this to be understood solely of material changes, for Aristotle expressly states that even the opinions of the philosophers themselves will recur in an identical form, " not once nor twice nor a few times but to infinity."[2]

[1] *Meteora*, I, xiv. I owe this and the following quotation to P. Duhem, *Le Système du Monde*, vols. I and II, in which the theories of Greek science regarding the Great Year are described in detail.
[2] *Met.*, I, iii.

On such an assumption the idea of progress must of course lose its meaning, since every movement of advance is at the same time a movement of return. Even the succession of time becomes a purely relative conception, as Aristotle himself very clearly shows. " If it is true that the Universe has a beginning, a middle and an end and that which has grown old and reached its end, has thereby returned anew to its beginning, and if the earlier things are those that are nearest to the beginning, what is there to prevent our being anterior to the men who lived in the time of the Trojan war? Alcmaeon has well said that men are mortal because they cannot join their end to their beginning. If the course of events is a circle, as the circle has neither beginning nor end, we cannot be anterior to the men of Troy and they cannot be anterior to us, since neither of us are nearer to the beginning."[1]

Not only is this point of view irreconcilable with a belief in progress, it seems to lead inevitably to the pessimistic fatalism of Ecclesiastes. " That which has been is that which shall be and that which has been done is that which shall be done : and there is no new thing under the sun. Is there a thing of which men say ' see this is new? ' It has been already in the ages that were before us."

And the same spirit dominates the thought of the Roman stoics, and inspires the fatalistic quietism of Marcus Aurelius. " The rational soul," he says, " traverses the whole universe and the surrounding void, and surveys its form and it extends itself into the infinity of time, and embraces and comprehends the periodical

[1] *Problemata*, XVII, 3.

renovation of all things, and it comprehends that those who come after us will see nothing new, nor have those before us seen anything more, but in a manner he who is forty years old, if he has any understanding at all, has seen, by virtue of the uniformity that prevails, all things that have been and all that will be.[1]

It is true that Aristotle tried to leave some room for contingency and free will, and denied the necessity of the numerical identity of mankind in the different cycles. But other thinkers were more thoroughgoing in their application of the theory. " According to the Pythagoreans," says Eudemus, " I shall be telling you the same story once more, holding the same staff in my hand, and you will be seated as you are at present, and all things will happen as before." And Stoics, like Zeno and Chrysippus, were equally uncompromising. When the cycle of the Great Year has completed its revolution, Dion will be here again, the same man in the same body, only excepting, says Chrysippus, such details as the wart upon his face! Indeed the philosophers of the Hellenistic age, went a step further, and taught that it was possible to foretell the next stage of the fated cycle from the study of the movements of the stars. We are so accustomed to think of Astrology as a popular superstition that we are apt to forget how closely it was bound up with ancient science and philosophy. The astrological fatalism of Manilius is nearer in spirit to modern scientific determinism than to popular superstition, and the Aristotelian theory that the movement of

---

[1] M. Aurel. Anton. XI, I.   Long's translation.   cf. Seneca *Ep. ad Lucilium* 24. *De tranquillitate* 1 and 2.

the heavens is the efficient cause of earthly change, seemed to provide a scientific basis for the most ambitious claims of the astrologers. Even the Neoplatonists, who were far less determinist than the other schools and preserved a high ideal of moral freedom and responsibility, did not deny the pre-established harmony between the events of the world below and the order of the heavens, though Plotinus conceived the stars not as causes, but as signs and ministers of the Eternal Mind.[1]

It is difficult to exaggerate the importance of these ideas in the history of ancient thought. They were not confined to a single age or to a single school. From the age of Pythagoras and Heraclitus down to the last days of the School of Athens under the Christian Emperors, the doctrine of the Great Year, and the recurrent cycle of cosmic change dominated the Greek mind. It is not that the Greeks were ignorant of the conception of progress. There is a long passage in the 5th book of Lucretius, derived no doubt from the writings of Epicurus himself, which describes the progress of humanity under the stimulus of the struggle for existence, from the purely animal conditions of its origin up to the highest achievements of civilized life, and which thus seems to anticipate the modern theory of evolutionary progress. But this idea does not dominate the thought of the poet. Behind it there lies the sombre pessimism of the Lucretian world view in which the whole life of mankind appears as a momentary spark, kindled and extinguished in the blind rush of falling atoms through infinite space and time. And even this qualified

[1] Cf. his long discussion of the subject in *Ennead*, II, iii, 7.

recognition of Progress is exceptional; elsewhere it is almost completely absent.

What is the reason of this state of things? It cannot be assigned to pessimism or to any falling off in the vigour and creative power of the Greek mind, for it is characteristic of Greek thought in its moments of triumphant achievement. Still less is it due to lack of knowledge. On the contrary it springs from the very nature of the Greek scientific ideal, which was impatient of partial solutions and had little in common with the laborious specialism of modern research. It aspired to know the cosmic process as a whole, and to render nature wholly transparent to the intelligence. But if intelligible law is to be supreme, there can be no room for the unique, incomparable historical event which seems to play so important a part in the world of experience. For a Greek to admit the reality of change was to deny the rationality of the universe. Sooner than take this step, he was prepared, with Parmenides, to deny the evidence of his senses, and to reject all change and becoming—even movement itself—as mere illusion. This, however, was equally fatal to a rational theory of nature since it explained the world of appearances only by abolishing it.

It was necessary to find some less drastic solution which would reconcile the process of phenomenal change with the unchanging unity of true Being. This was the achievement of Empedocles who first found the way which Greek thought was henceforward to follow. He asserted no less strongly than Parmenides that what *is* cannot perish and that what *is not* can never come into being. There is however

147

a perpetual cycle of change by which the One becomes the Many and the Many pass into the One. "They prevail in turn as the circle comes round, and pass into one another and grow great in their appointed turn." "Thus in so far as they are wont to grow into one out of many, and, again divided, become more than one, so far they come into being and their life is not lasting; but in so far as they never cease changing continually, so far are they evermore, immovable in the circle."[1]

[1] Empedocles fr. 26, tr. Burnet, *Early Greek Philosophy*, p. 244 2nd ed.

VII

CHRISTIANITY AND THE RISE OF WESTERN CIVILIZATION

WE have seen that the great movement of thought which passed over the ancient world about the middle of the first millennium B.C. tended to turn away men's minds from the world of human experience to the contemplation of absolute and unchanging Being, from Time to Eternity. There was, however, one important exception to this tendency. In the development of Hebrew religion the influence of metaphysical speculation is almost negligible, and there was no attempt to transcend the social order or to deny the importance of the temporal and historical process. Moreover, the religion of Israel differed from the normal type of world religion in several other respects. All the other world religions were linked with some great historic culture whose traditions they had incorporated. Even the Greeks had behind them the very ancient and highly developed cultural tradition of the Ægean world, while in India and China the connection of the new religious movement with a great autonomous culture tradition is even more obvious. The religion of Israel, on the other hand, was based on practically no material foundation.

149

It belonged to a minor people which occupied a very limited territory, and one which was neither rich nor highly civilized. Unlike the Greeks or the Aryans in India, the Hebrews had not conquered or incorporated a whole civilization. They had merely gained a rather precarious foothold among the older peoples of the Near East, and on every side they were exposed to the influence of more highly developed and more powerful cultures.

It is not that Israel was without any contact with the archaic culture. On the contrary Palestine was saturated with Babylonian and Egyptian influences, and even the holy places of the Hebrew religious tradition—Sinai, Mt. Nebo, Beth-Shemesh, etc., bear the names of Babylonian divinities. But this environment was hostile rather than favourable to the new religion. The religious tradition of Israel was that of a warrior nomad people. Their god was not a city god, like Baal of Tyre, or a peaceful deity of the farm and the harvest, like Tammuz, but the god of storm and battle, whom we see in the splendid battle song preserved in the book of Habakkuk, coming up out of the mountains and the southern desert to destroy his enemies and to judge his people. Contact with the higher civilization of the settled lands always tended to weaken the spiritual independence of the people and to contaminate the purity of the religion of Jahweh with the licentious and immoral cults of the Syrian vegetation religion.

Thus the history of Israel shows how a lower and more barbaric material culture may become the vehicle of a higher religious tradition. For Jahweh was not only a war god, he was the god of righteousness and truth, and the supremacy of the ethical element in Hebrew religion was due to the uncompromising and intolerant spirit which turned away from the higher culture of the cities of Canaan and looked to Sinai and the desert.

Nevertheless, in Israel, no less than in the case of other world religions, the new religious development was based on the idea of a ritual order. The sacred temple city of Jerusalem with its priesthood and its ceremonial order also took a fundamental part in the history of Jewish religion. Indeed, there is no other case in which the spiritual life of a people is bound up so closely with ritual conceptions, and the whole ethical and social development is so directly based upon a sacred ceremonial order. In Israel, however, this divine law which governed both the moral life of the individual and the external organization of society was never conceived as an impersonal cosmic order, such as we find in Greek or Chinese thought. It was always regarded as the Word and ordinance of a personal deity, Jahweh, the God of Israel.

Now there is nothing peculiar in the fact that the people of Israel should have owned allegiance to a single god. That was more or less the normal state of things among ancient peoples, and especially among the Semites. There was Assur, the national god of Assyria, Chemosh, the god of Moab, the great Baal of Tyre, and countless others. But these were often merely the heads of a whole pantheon of minor deities, and in almost all cases they were accompanied by a female companion or consort such as Ishtar, or the Ashtoreth of the Bible, for the sexual element entered deeply into ancient religion, and the more civilized the people the stronger, as a rule, was the emphasis on this aspect of life. The God of Israel, on the other hand, tolerated no companion. He was a jealous God, who hated the licentious cultus of the native agricultural and city dwelling population of Canaan. Consequently, while the general tendency in the new age was to syncretize the various local cults and to subordinate all these personal divinities to some transcendent impersonal principle such as Brahman, the tendency in Israel was to accentuate the unity and the universality of the national god.[1]

This tendency already appears fully developed in the 8th century in the earliest prophetic writings. In the book of Amos, Jahweh is not a mere national deity whose power is limited to his own people and land. He is the god of the whole earth " who maketh the Pleiades and Orion and turneth the shadow of death into the morning and maketh the day dark with night." " He that formeth the mountains and createth the wind and declareth unto man what is his thought, that maketh the morning darkness and treadeth on the high places of the earth." And no less striking is the emphasis laid upon the moral and spiritual character of Jahweh's rule. He has no pleasure in the external observances of the national cult. He hates and despises the sacrifices of the oppressors of the poor. His law is to " hate the evil and love the good and to establish judgment in the gate."

Consequently when the Assyrian world power conquered the lesser people of the Near East, the

---

[1] The only other example of this tendency is to be found in the Zoroastrian religion of Persia which in several respects offers a remarkable parallel to the Jewish development.

religion of Jahweh did not share the political fortunes of the nation, as was the case with the other peoples. For the prophets saw in the material ruin of Israel not a proof of the powerlessness of Jahweh to protect his people, but a manifestation of his universal power in a higher and more mysterious sense. Assyria itself was but an instrument in the hand of the God of Israel, which would be discarded and broken when his purpose was accomplished, and Israel was to look for salvation not to " the arm of the flesh," but to the mysterious workings of divine omnipotence.

Thus the crisis which destroyed the existence of Israel as an independent nation was also the time of travail in which Judaism was reborn as a world religion. The series of national calamities which culminated in the destruction of Jerusalem and the period of the captivity only strengthened and enlarged the prophetic belief in the sovereignty of the divine purpose in history. And this purpose was no longer limited to the fate of Israel himself, it had an even wider significance. " It is too light a thing that thou shouldest be my servant to raise up the tribes of Jacob and to restore the preserved of Israel; I will also give thee for a light to the Gentiles, that thou mayest be my salvation unto the end of the earth " (Isaiah xlix. 6). The sufferings of Israel and of the Chosen Servant of Jahweh were the necessary means by which God's power and righteousness were to be manifested to humanity. From the beginning the will of Jahweh had set apart this little Palestinian people as his chosen vehicle, and the great world empires which had crushed Israel in the dust of their advance were but the instruments of this transcendent purpose. Thus all history was moving to a great consummation, the revelation of the power and glory of Jahweh in his servant Israel, and the eternal reign of justice in the Messianic kingdom of God.

Consequently, to the Jews, history possessed a unique and absolute value such as no other people of antiquity had conceived. The eternal law which the Greeks saw embodied in the ordered movement of the heavens was manifested to the Jews in the vicissitudes of human history. While the philosophers of India and Greece were meditating on the illusoriness or the eternity of the cosmic process, the prophets of Israel were affirming the moral purpose in history and were interpreting the passing events of their age as the revelation of the divine will. For them there could be no question of the return of all things in an eternal cycle of cosmic change, since the essence of their doctrine of the divine purpose in the world was its uniqueness. There was one God and one Israel, and in the relations between these two was comprised the whole purpose of creation. And so when, in the course of history, the Jews were brought into relation with the cosmopolitan culture of the Hellenistic age, they alone preserved their own religious tradition and their own view of the world, and entrenched themselves behind the barrier of an ever stricter observance of the traditional ritual order. It is true that they did not entirely escape the influence of the dominant idea of a cyclic process in the world order, but they reinterpreted this conception in the spirit of their own tradition. The æon of Jewish apocalyptic is not a true cycle, it is a stage in the development of a single process, which retains its unique value and importance.

It is, however, transferred from the historical to the cosmic plane, or rather transformed into that species of cosmic history which we know as apocalyptic.

It was to this prophetic and apocalyptic tradition, as distinct from the legal ritualism which formed the other element in the Jewish heritage that the new religious movement which was destined to transform the ancient world made its appeal. Both the social and the cosmic elements of that tradition were represented in its teaching, but they acquired a new spiritual and mystical significance. The Kingdom of God appears in the Gospels as at once a fulfilment of the ancient prophecies of the restoration of Israel, and as a new world order which would renew heaven and earth, but it was also a new life, a transforming leaven, a seed in the heart of man. And the source of the new order was found, not in a mythological figure, like the Saviour Gods of the Mystery Religions, nor in an abstract cosmic principle, but in the historical personality of Jesus, the crucified Nazarene. For Christianity taught that in Jesus a new principle of divine life had entered the human race and the natural world by which mankind is raised to a higher order. Christ is the head of this restored humanity, the firstborn of the new creation, and the life of the Church consists in the progressive extension of the Incarnation by the gradual incorporation of mankind into this higher unity. Hence the Absolute and the Finite, the Eternal and the Temporal, God and the World were no longer conceived as two exclusive and opposed orders of being standing over against one another in mutual isolation. The two orders interpenetrated one another, and even the lower world of matter and sense was

155

capable of becoming the vehicle and channel of the divine life.

Thus the Jewish affirmation of the significance and value of history found a yet wider development in Christianity. The world process was conceived not as an unchanging order governed by the fatal law of necessity, but as a divine drama whose successive acts were the Creation and Fall of Man, his Redemption, and his glorious restoration.

Hence, in spite of the Christian opposition between " This World " and " The World to Come," there could be no tampering with the reality and uniqueness of the historical process. The irreconcilability of Christianity with the dominant theory of cosmic cycles is obvious, and was stated uncompromisingly by the early Fathers. " If we accept that theory," says Origen, " then Adam and Eve will do in a second world exactly as they have done in this: the same deluge will be repeated; the same Moses will bring the same people out of Egypt, Judas will a second time betray his Lord, and again Paul will keep the garments of those who will stone Stephen."[1]

And it was on this very ground that the Church had to fight its earliest battles, for Gnosticism was essentially an attempt to combine the belief in spiritual redemption with the theory of world-æons and of the illusory nature of earthly change, and consequently the whole anti-Gnostic apologia of St. Irenaeus is directed to the defence of the value and reality of the historical development. " Since men are real, theirs must be a real establishment. They do not vanish into non-existence, but progress among existent things."

[1] *Peri archon* lib II, ch. iii, 4-5. Cf. St. Aug., *de Civ. Dei*, XII, 13.

" There is one Son who performs the Father's will, and one human race in which the mysteries of God are realised." " God arranged everything from the first with a view to the perfection of man, in order to deify him and reveal His own dispensations, so that goodness may be made manifest, justice made perfect, and the Church may be fashioned after the image of His Son. Thus man may eventually reach maturity, and, being ripened by such privileges, may see and comprehend God."[1]

It was to this consciousness of its unique character and mission that Christianity owes its extraordinary powers of expansion and conquest which revolutionized the whole development of Western civilization. For it cannot be too strongly insisted that the victory of the Church in the 4th century was not, as so many modern critics would have us believe, the natural culmination of the religious evolution of the ancient world. It was, on the contrary, a violent interruption of that process which forced European civilization out of its old orbit into a path which it would never have followed by its own momentum. It is true that the classical culture and the religion of the city state with which it was associated were losing their vitality, and that nothing could have arrested the movement of orientalization which ultimately conquered the Roman world. But this movement found its normal expression either in the undiluted form which is represented by the different Gnostic and Manichæan sects, or in a bastard Hellenistic syncretism. The religion of the Emperor Julian and his Neoplatonist teachers, in spite of their devotion to the Hellenic

[1] St. Irenaeus, *Against Heresies*, V, 36, 1. IV, 37, 7. Tr. F. M. Hitchcock.

157

past was actually more impregnated with oriental elements than was that of the Christian Fathers, such as Eusebius of Cæsarea, Theodore of Mopsuestia, Theodoret, Basil and the two Gregories.

For the writings of the latter, in spite of their avowed hostility to the Greek religious tradition, were characterized by a genuine spirit of humanism, for which there was little room in the spiritualistic theosophy of Julian and Maximus of Tyre. Their whole apologetic is dominated by the conception of Man as the centre and crown of the created universe. The first book of the *Theophany* of Eusebius is a long panegyric of humanity,—man the craftsman and artist, the builder of cities and the sailor of ships,—man the scientist and philosopher who alone can foretell the changes of the heavenly bodies and knows the hidden causes of things,—man a God upon earth, " the dear child of the Divine Word."

So, too, St. Gregory of Nyssa sees in man not only " the god-like image of the archetypal beauty," but the channel through which the whole material creation acquires consciousness and becomes spiritualized and united to God. Just as in the material world itself, he says, there is an inner organic harmony of creation, so, too, there is, by the Divine wisdom, a certain commingling of the intelligible world with the sensible creation, so that no part of creation might be rejected or deprived of Divine fellowship. And the bond of this mixture and communion is to be found in human nature. Man was created by God " in order that the earthly element might be raised by union with the Divine, and so the Divine grace in one even course, as it were, might uniformly extend through all creation, the lower nature being mingled with that which is above the world."[1] This created nature, however, is essentially changeable. It continually passes through a process of evolution, which so long as it acts in accordance with nature will always be progressive, but which, on the other hand, may become a movement of degeneration and decline, if once the will should become perverted.[2]

This is what has happened in the actual history of humanity, and therefore it has been necessary for the Divine Nature to unite itself with mankind in a second creation which will restore and still further develop the original function of humanity. Thus the Incarnation is the source of a new movement of regeneration and progress which leads ultimately to the deification of human nature by its participation in the Divine Life. The life of the Divine Trinity externalizes itself in the Church as the restored humanity, and the purpose of creation finds its complete fulfilment in the Incarnate Word, " Who unites the universe to Himself, bringing in His own Person the different kinds of existing things to one accord and harmony."[3]

This presentation of the Christian doctrine of man and the Incarnation is a conscious attempt to express the new Christian world view in a form accessible to the Greek mind. It is a genuine synthesis of the Christian and the Platonic traditions, and one which, in spite of Harnack's criticism, is in entire agreement with the spirit of St. Paul himself. Nevertheless, the Hellenic tradition to which Eusebius and St. Gregory

---

[1] St. Gregory Nyssen. *Cathetical Discourse*, *cap* VI., trans. J. H. Srawley, p. 39.
[2] *Id. cap* VIII.   [3] *Id. cap* XXXII.

addressed themselves was not the dominant force in the world of the day. At the same time that the Church was successfully carrying on its apostolate in the Græco-Roman world, it was itself being assailed in the rear by the orientalizing heresies which sought to convert Christianity into a religion of pure spirit, and asserted that the body and the material world were essentially evil. This force not only manifested itself in forms such as Manichæanism and Gnosticism, which were the open enemies of orthodox Christianity, but also made itself felt within the Church by the influence of Encratite works such as the apocryphal Gospels and Acta, as well as by the Monophysite tendency which denied the orthodox doctrine of the full humanity of Christ, and which saw in the Incarnation only the appearance upon earth of the divinity in bodily form.

Consequently the Byzantine culture does not simply represent the fusion of the Hellenistic-Roman tradition with Christianity. It contains a third element of oriental origin which is, in fact, the preponderant influence in Byzantine civilization. It is to be seen in the social and political organization of the Empire which borrowed from Sassanian Persia all the external forms of the oriental sacred monarchy. The rigid hierarchy of the Byzantine state which centres in the Sacred Palace and the quasi-divine person of the Holy Emperor is neither Roman nor Christian, but purely oriental. And the same influence is to be seen in Byzantine religion in its tendency to neglect the historical and dynamic element in the Christian tradition, and to become absorbed in theological speculations regarding the nature of the Godhead. This tendency reaches its climax in the writings of the so-called

Dionysius the Areopagite, which probably date from the close of the 5th century, and have exerted an incalculable influence on the religious life of the Byzantine world. Here we may see the most extreme assertion of the Divine Transcendence and the negation of all finite modes of being.

" As intelligible things are not to be comprehended by the senses . . . so, too, the infinite Super-Being transcends Being, the Super-intelligible unity transcends Intelligences, the One that is beyond thought transcends comprehension, and the Good which is beyond speech transcends expression. For it is a Monad which unifies every unity, a Super-essential Essence, an Unintelligible Mind, an Ineffable Word, or rather the negation of Reason, Intelligence, Word, and every particular form of existence."[1]

Consequently in order to attain to the knowledge of this Divine Negation " man must plunge into the mystical darkness of Unknowing in which he lays aside all rational knowledge and becomes absorbed in that which is wholly intangible and invisible . . . so that he is united to that which is wholely unknowable by the highest part of the mind in the complete cessation of rational knowledge and knows in a manner beyond mind by knowing nothing."[2]

But this way of absolute negation is not the whole of the Dionysian teaching. It is supplemented by the theory of a mystical hierarchy, by which the initiate is gradually led upwards by a series of ritual acts and sacramental symbols from the Sensible to the Intelligible and from the Intelligible to the Divine.

[1] *On the Divine Names*, i. i.
[2] *The Mystical Theology*, i. 3.

Thus abstract mysticism is linked up with a fixed ritual and ceremonial order which is its earthly and sensible counterpart: in his own words " the Theurgy is the completion of the Theology."[1]

Similarly the moral ideal of the Byzantine world found its expression in the uncompromising other-worldliness of the monks of the desert which represents the extreme development of the oriental spirit of asceticism and world-denial within the boundaries of orthodox Christianity. For the naked fasting ascetics of Nitria and the Thebaid, the state and the world of social duties had ceased to exist. They had cut themselves off from all social ties; they recognised no political obligation. They lived entirely for the spirit, and left the body nothing save the right of bare existence.

Nevertheless, even this radically oriental version of Christianity did not satisfy the Eastern world. With the coming of Islam it reverted to a simpler type of religion, which felt no need for any incarnation of the divine or any progressive transformation of human nature. The bridge between God and Man was broken, and the Divine Omnipotence once more reigned in lonely splendour, like the sun over the desert.

In the Roman West, in spite of its lower standard of civilization, the conditions were more favourable to the development of an original and creative Christian culture. For here the Church did not become incorporated in a fixed social and political order which it was powerless to modify; it found itself abandoned to its own resources in a world of chaos and destruction.

[1] *The Ecclesiastical Hierarchy*, III, 3, 5.

It had to contend, not with the influence of an alien spiritual tradition, but with the forces of barbarism and social disorder. But long before the fall of the Empire, Western Catholicism had already acquired the distinctive characteristics that were to mark its future development. The oldest document of Western Christianity—the First Epistle of Clement—already shows the Latin sense of order and its practical ideal of social duty. Even the Western heresies from the days of Novatian and the Donatists to Pelagius and Priscillian are not concerned with speculative theology, but with the concrete matters of Church order or with the problems of moral conduct and moral responsibility.

Moreover the emphasis on the social aspect of the Christian tradition led the Western Church to assume a much more independent attitude to the state than that of the Byzantine Church. Hilary of Poitiers, in the reign of Constantine, attacks the interference of the state in religious matters with a vehemence that is hardly surpassed by the champions of the mediæval Papacy, and St. Ambrose, in his relations with the Christian Emperors, affirms the authority of the spiritual power in the spirit of a mediæval pontiff rather than a Byzantine prelate. The Emperor, he says, is within the Church, not above it, and consequently it is the duty of the Christian ruler to subordinate his action to the Church's decrees in all matters that concern the faith.

But it was St. Augustine who first gave a more profound philosophical and theological orientation to the genius of the Western Church. It is true that his thought was by no means free of oriental elements. It was not for nothing that he had been for years a disciple of the Manichæans, and that his mind had also been permeated by the influence of Neoplatonism. He was dominated by that nostalgia of the infinite which led the thinkers of the oriental world to turn away from the world of experience towards the eternal vision of transcendent Being. Nevertheless he was also a Latin, and his Latin sense of social and historical reality led him to do justice to the social and historical elements that are implicit in the Christian tradition. His ideal was not an impersonal Nirvana, but the City of God, and he saw the spiritual order not as a static metaphysical principle, but as a dynamic force which manifests itself in human society. Two loves, he says, built two cities. The love of Self builds up Babylon to the contempt of God, and the love of God builds up Jerusalem to the contempt of Self. All history consists of the evolution of these principles embodied in two societies, " blended one with another and moving on in all changes of times from the beginning of the human race even to the end of the world."[1]

Consequently the present world is neither a complete static order nor an unmeaning and illusory appearance. It is the birth process of a spiritual creation, the seminal or embryonic activity of a new life. And the actuating principle in this process is the Divine Spirit which manifests itself in the world, outwardly through the sacramental order of the Church, and inwardly in the soul by the operation of the spiritual will. For St. Augustine's emphasis on the weakness of human nature and the omnipotence of divine grace does not imply any under-valuing of the ethical aspect of life.

[1] *de Catechizandis rudibus* 37.

On the contrary, paradoxical as it may seem, it was the importance that he attached to the moral will that led him to depreciate its freedom. The human will is the engine that God employs for the creation of a new world.

Thus while Christianity in the East tended to become a speculative mysticism embodied in a system of ritual —a μυσταγωγία in the technical sense—in the West, under the influence of Augustine, it became a dynamic moral and social force. This is the distinction which Ritschl stated so forcibly in his comparison of St. Augustine with the Pseudo-Areopagite. The latter, he says, was the founder of a ritual ecclesiasticism, the former of an ecclesiasticism of moral tasks in the service of a world-wide Christianity. It is true that this aspect of Western Christianity can easily be exaggerated. St. Augustine was not an Americanist. He did not value the active moral life as an end in itself. He realized as fully as any oriental the supremacy of the transcendent and the ideal of mystical contemplation. But while the East concentrated itself on this aspect of religion to the exclusion of all else, the spirit of the Western Church is expressed in the great words of the dying St. Martin: " Domine si populo tuo adhuc sum necessarius, *non recuso laborem.*"

This is the spirit which inspired the Western Church in the age of darkness and anarchy which followed the downfall of the Empire. It is to be seen in the work of the Papacy, as represented above all by St. Gregory, who laboured amidst the ruins of a dying civilization to serve the cause of social justice and humanity. It is to be seen no less in the new Benedictine monasticism which converted the purely ascetic tradition of the monks of the desert into a disciplined social institution in the service of the Universal Church. These two powers were the chief and almost the only constructive social forces in Western Europe during the Dark Ages. It was they who reunited England to Christendom and created a new centre of Christian and Latin culture in the North. And it was the Saxon monks, such as Willibrord and Boniface and Alcuin who, in close alliance with the Papacy, converted heathen Germany, reformed the Frankish church, and laid the foundations of the Carolingian culture.

Hence the new civilization which slowly and painfully began to emerge in the early middle ages was in a very special sense a religious creation, for it was based on an ecclesiastical not a political unity. While in the East, the imperial unity was still all-inclusive and the Church was essentially the Church of the Empire, in the West it was the Church that was the universal society and the state was weak, barbarous and divided. The only true citizenship that remained to the common man was his membership of the Church, and it involved a far deeper and wider loyalty than his allegiance to the secular state. It was the fundamental social relation which overrode all distinctions of class and nationality. The Church was a world in itself, with its own culture, its own organization and its own law. In so far as civilization survived, it was directly dependent on the Church, whether in the great Carolingian monasteries, such as St. Gall or Fulda, which were the chief centres of cultural and economic life, or in the cities which came to depend on the bishops and the ecclesiastical element for their very existence. The state, on the other hand, had become divorced

166

from the city and the civic culture and reverted more and more to the warlike traditions of a barbarous tribal aristocracy.

For mediæval Europe no longer possessed a homogeneous material culture, such as we find, for example, in China or India. It was a loose federation of the most diverse types of race and culture under the hegemony of a common religious and ecclesiastical tradition. This explains the contradictions and disunity of mediæval culture—the contrast of its cruelty and its charity, its beauty and squalor, its spiritual vitality and its material barbarism. For the element of higher culture did not spring naturally from the traditions of the social organism itself, but came in from outside as a spiritual power which had to remould and transform the social material in which it attempted to embody itself.

And so in the 11th and 12th centuries, when the social revival of Western Europe began, the new development was inspired by religious motives, and proceeded directly from the tradition of the spiritual society. The struggle of the Investitures and the international supremacy of the reformed Papacy were the visible signs of the victory of the spiritual power over the feudal and barbaric elements in European society. Everywhere men became conscious of their common citizenship in the great religious commonwealth of Christendom. And this spiritual citizenship was the foundation of a new society. As members of the feudal state, men were separated by the countless divisions of allegiance and jurisdiction. They were parcelled out like sheep with the land, on which they lived, among different lordships. But as members of the Church, they met on a common ground. "Before Christ," writes St. Ivo of Chartres, "there is neither free man nor serf, all who participate in the same sacraments are equal."

And, in fact, a new democratic spirit of brotherhood and social co-operation begins to make itself felt in Europe at this epoch. In every walk of life men leagued themselves together in voluntary associations for social objects under religious auspices. The main types of association were three in number: the sworn "peace" for the enforcement of the Truce of God and the suppression of brigandage; the fellowship of the road, which pilgrims or merchants entered into for mutual protection; and the confraternity or "Charité," a local union for charitable or social objects under the patronage of some popular saint. From these origins there sprang the great movement of communal activity which transformed the social life of mediæval Europe. It was no longer based exclusively on military service and feudal subordination. It was a vast complex of social organisms, a federation of corporate bodies, each of which possessed an independent activity, and made its own contribution to the common weal. The national kingdom itself was conceived as a federation of different orders, each with its own social function—the Estates of the Realm.

And the same tendency is equally active in the ecclesiastical sphere. The socialization of monasticism in the service of the universal Church which had been begun by the Benedictines, was carried still further in the new period. The reform of the Church in the 11th century was to a great extent a monastic movement, in which, for the first time, the monks were impelled by the force of their own ideals to leave the peace of the cloister and to throw themselves into a semi-political struggle. And in the following century the life of St. Bernard shows how the strictest ideals of monastic asceticism were not inconsistent with a social activity which embraced every aspect of the international life of Christendom. Henceforward the monastery is no longer a self-contained society with no relations to the outer world. It forms part of a wider unity, the Order, which in turn is an organ of the universal Church. And the new ideal finds a still more complete expression in the mendicant orders which arose in the 13th century, such as the Franciscans and the Dominicans. Here the ideal of service entirely replaces the old aim of retirement from the world. The friars are no longer bound to the rigid uniformity of cloistered life, they are free to go anywhere and do anything which the needs of the Church requires. They answer to the needs of the new civic life, with its communal activity, as the fixed territorial abbey did to those of the old feudal agrarian state.

Thus by the 13th century Christendom had organized itself as a vast international unity founded on an ecclesiastical rather than a political basis. This unity, moreover, was not confined to purely religious matters, it embraced the whole of social life. All education and literary culture, all art, all matters of social welfare, such as the relief of the poor and the care of the sick, fell within the Church's sphere of influence. It even exercised a direct influence on war and politics, since the Papacy was the supreme arbiter in any question in which the interests of religion or justice were at stake, and since it could launch the armies of Christendom in a crusade against the enemies of the faith or those who disregarded the rights of the Church.

It might seem as though Europe was destined to become a theocratic Church-state, after the manner of Islam, with the Pope as the Commander of the Faithful. And, indeed, there was a real danger that as the Church succeeded in dominating the state, it would itself be secularized by the growth of wealth and political power, until it became a legal rather than a spiritual organization. This danger was, however, counteracted by the spiritual revival which accompanied the social and intellectual renaissance of the 12th century. The dynamic moral energy of the Augustinian tradition continued to characterize Western Catholicism, and found expression in a new and more personal type of piety. The humanity of Christ became the centre of the religious life in a sense in which it had never been before. In place of the severe figure of the Byzantine Christ, throned in awful majesty as ruler and judge of men, there appears the figure of the Saviour in His human weakness and passibility. This attempt to enter into a close personal relationship with the Divine Humanity gives birth to a kind of religious realism which is very different from the abstract theological piety of the patristic and Byzantine types. We see this already in the writings of St. Bernard, but it is in the life and teaching of St. Francis that the new spirit finds its fullest development. The ideal of St. Francis is to relive the life of Christ in the experience of daily life. There is no longer any separation between faith and life, or between the spiritual and the material, since the two worlds have become fused together in the living reality of practical experience. And so, too, the asceticism of St. Francis no longer involves the rejection of the natural world and the turning away of the mind from the created to the Absolute. The rule of Poverty is a means of liberation, not a movement of negation. It brings man back to the fellowship of God's creation which had been lost or vitiated by self-will.

The powers of nature which had been first divinized and worshipped, and then in turn rejected by man as he realized the transcendence of the spiritual, are now brought back into the world of religion, and in his great canticle of the sun, St. Francis once more celebrates the praises of Mother Earth, the bearer of fruit, who keeps and sustains us, Brother Fire, who is " fair and joyous and mighty and strong," and all the other holy creatures of God. Thus the Franciscan attitude to nature and human life marks a turning point in the religious history of the West. It is the end of the long period during which human nature and the present world had been dwarfed and immobilized by the shadow of eternity, and the beginning of a new epoch of humanism and interest in nature. As Karl Burdach has shown, its importance is not limited to the religious field, but it has a wider significance for the whole development of European culture. Its influence is to be seen both in the new art of 13th and 14th century Italy, which already contains the germs of the Renaissance, and in the social movements of the 14th century, in which for the first time the poorest and most oppressed elements of mediæval society asserted their claims to justice.

But it is in the region of thought that the new realization of the reality and value of humanity and the whole order of nature had the most important results. The

171

great intellectual synthesis of the 13th century has often been regarded as the triumph of theological dogmatism. It was in reality the assertion of the rights of the human reason and the foundation of European science. As Harnack has said, " Scholasticism is nothing else but scientific thought," and its weakness in the sphere of natural science is simply due to the fact that there was as yet no body of observed facts upon which it could exercise itself.[1] Greek science, as embodied in the writings of Aristotle, represented a level of scientific achievement far higher than anything which the mediæval world could attain to by its unaided powers, and consequently it was taken over *en bloc* by the scholastic movement. It was, however, no small achievement to succeed in bringing this mass of knowledge into living relation with mediæval culture. Greek science belonged to the Greek world, and it is not easy to transplant it into another world ruled by a different vital rhythm, and inspired by different moral and religious principles. This was the experience of the Islamic world where the same experiment was made with no less enthusiasm and with a considerably higher endowment of cultural tradition than in the West. In Islam, however, the internal conflict between the scientific and the religious traditions proved incapable of solution. The Moslem thinker who in genius and influence most resembles St. Thomas —Ghazali—devoted his powers to " the destruction of philosophy "[2] rather than to its reconciliation with

---

[1] He adds, " The science of the Middle Ages gives practical proof of eagerness in thinking, and exhibits an energy in subjecting all that is real and valuable to thought, to which we can find perhaps no parallel in any other age." *History of Dogma* (Eng. tr.), vol. VI, p. 25.
[2] His most famous work is entitled *Tehâfut el Falâsifah* " *The Destruction of the Philosophers.*"

faith, and this not because he was a mere obscurantist, but because he saw more clearly than his opponents the fundamental incompatibility of the central Moslem doctrine of the divine omnipotence with the Hellenic conception of the universe as an intelligible order which is transparent to the human reason.

In the West the relations between religion and philosophy were different because the former was based on an historical rather than a metaphysical revelation. The provinces of faith and reason did not coincide, they were complementary and not contradictory. Each had its own *raison d'etre* and its own sphere of activity. Against the oriental religions of absolute being and pure spirit, with their tendency to deny the reality or the value of the material world, Christianity had undeviatingly maintained the dignity of humanity, and the value of the material element in man's nature.

Hitherto, however, Christian thought had not fully realized the implications of this doctrine. The predominance of oriental influences had led to a concentration on the spiritual side of man's nature; its ideal was "to pass beyond sensible things and to become united to the divine and the intelligible by the power of the intelligence."[1] It was the work of the new philosophy, as represented above all by St. Thomas, for the first time to break with the old established tradition of oriental spiritualism and Neoplatonic idealism, and to bring man back into the order of nature. He taught that the human intelligence is not that of a pure spirit, it is consubstantial with matter, and finds its natural activity in the sphere of the sensible and the particular.

[1] S. Athanasius *Contra Gentes* ii.

173

Consequently man cannot attain in this life to the direct intuition of truth and spiritual reality. He must build up an intelligible world slowly and painfully from the data of the senses, ordered and systematized by science, until at last the intelligible order which is inherent in created things is disengaged from the envelope of matter and contemplated in its relation to the absolute Being by the light of the higher intelligence.

Thus, looked at from one point of view, man is so low in the scale of creation, so deeply sunk in animality as hardly to deserve the title of an intellectual being. Even the rational activity of which he is so proud, is a distinctively *animal* form of intellect, and can only arise where the higher intelligence is veiled and impeded by the conditions of space and time.[1] On the other hand man occupies a unique position in the universe precisely because he is the lowest of all spiritual natures. He is the point at which the world of spirit touches the world of sense, and it is through him and in him that the material creation attains to intelligibility and becomes enlightened and spiritualized.

Man is, as it were, a God upon earth, since it is his function to reduce the unintelligible chaos of the world of phenomena to reason and order. But he is so bound to matter that he is himself in continual danger of being dragged down to the purely animal life of the senses and passions. And since he cannot free himself by transcending the conditions of his nature in an intellectual approach to the world of pure spirit, the Divine Word has manifested itself to man through the

[1] Ratio nihil est nisi natura intellectualis adumbrata. *Comment in Sententias* I D III Q IV a 1. Rationale est differentia animalis et Deo non convenit nec Angelis. *Id.* I D XXV QI a 1.

sensible and the concrete in a form which is appropriate to the limitations of his intellectual powers. Thus the Incarnation does not destroy or supersede nature. It is analogous and complementary to it, since it restores and extends man's natural function as the bond of union between the material and the spiritual worlds. This is the fundamental principle of the synthesis of St. Thomas. His whole work is governed by the desire to show the concordance in difference of the two orders. Alike in his epistemology, his ethics and his politics, St. Thomas emphasizes the rights and the autonomous character of natural activity, the province of Reason as distinct from that of Faith, the moral law of Nature as distinct from that of Grace, the rights of the State as distinct from those of the Church.

It is true that St. Thomas had no intention of turning men's minds away from the spiritual world to the study of particular and contingent being. His philosophic ideal, as Père Rousselot has shown,[1] is emphatically an absolute intellectualism, and he regards the science of the sensible world merely as the lowest rung in a ladder which leads the mind step by step to the contemplation of eternal truth. Nevertheless the new appreciation of the rights of nature and reason which his philosophy involved marked a turning point in the history of European thought. The human mind was no longer absorbed in the contemplation of the eternal and the unchanging, it was set free to take up once more its natural task of the material organization of the world by science and law.

But it is obvious that St. Thomas himself and the men of his generation had no conception of the vast-

---

[1] In *L'intellectualisme de St. Thomas* 2nd ed. 1924.

ness and complexity of the problem. Their synthesis was regarded as final and complete, since they could not foresee that the advance of scientific knowledge would lead to the entire reconstruction of Aristotelian physics. As soon as the European mind began to exploit the riches of knowledge and power that the world contained, it began to turn away from the intellectualism of St. Thomas towards a purely rational or empirical ideal of knowledge. In every department of life the later Middle Ages witnessed a reaction from the idealism of the old religious culture. In philosophy, nominalism and criticism were triumphant, in art, realism took the place of abstract symbolism. In politics and social life, the unity of mediæval Christendom was being broken up by the growing forces of nationalism and secular culture. The new peoples of the West in the pride and vigour of youth were preparing to emancipate themselves from ecclesiastical tutelage and to set about creating an independent cultural life of their own.

VIII

THE SECULARIZATION OF WESTERN CULTURE AND THE RISE OF THE RELIGION OF PROGRESS

THE civilization of mediæval Christendom was essentially dependent on the ecclesiastical organization of Europe as an international or rather supernational unity. It was irreconcilable with the conception of a number of completely independent sovereign societies such as the national states of modern Europe. The mediæval state was a congeries of semi-independent principalities and corporations, each of which enjoyed many of the attributes of sovereignty, while all of them together formed part of a wider society—the Christian people. As we have seen, however, this wider unity did not possess the social and cultural homogeneity of the great oriental civilizations, such as China. It incorporated and overlaid a number of distinct earlier culture traditions, such as those of the Latin culture of the Mediterranean, and the more barbarous tribal societies of Northern Europe. This underlying diversity of cultural tradition expressed itself in the awakening of the national spirit and the formation of separate national cultures which reached their full development in the age of the Renaissance and the Reformation. The mediæval unity was torn in sunder by a centrifugal

177

movement, which made itself felt alike in culture, in religion, and in political and ecclesiastical organization.

In the South this movement took the form of a return to the older tradition of culture. The Renaissance in Italy was not a mere revival of scholarly interests in a dead past, as was usually the case in the northern countries. It was a true national awakening. Men saw the revival of classical learning as the recovery of a lost inheritance. They revolted against the mediæval culture not on religious grounds but because it was alien and uncivilized. They entered on a crusade to free the Latin world from the yoke of Gothic barbarism.

In Northern Europe it is obvious that the movement of national awakening had to find a different form of expression, since there was here no older tradition of higher culture, and behind the mediæval period there lay an age of pagan barbarism. Consequently Northern Europe could only assert its cultural independence by a remoulding and transforming of the Christian tradition itself in accordance with its national genius. The Renaissance of Northern Europe is the Reformation.

The situation was not unlike that of the subject oriental nationalities of the Roman Empire in the 5th and 6th centuries. Just as, in the latter case, the religious revolt of Syria and Egypt against the Imperial Church represents a national reaction of the oriental element against the dominance of the Hellenistic-Roman culture, so, in the Reformation, we may see a Nordic revolt against the Latin traditions of the mediæval culture. The syncretism of Roman and Germanic elements which had been achieved by the Carolingian age, was terminated by a violent explosion which separated the mediæval culture complex into its component elements, and reorganized them on new lines. Thus the Reformation is the parallel and complement of the Renaissance; as the one made the culture of Southern Europe more purely Latin, so the other made the culture of Northern Europe more purely Teutonic.

Hence it is no mere coincidence that the line of religious division after the Reformation follows so closely that of the old imperial frontier. On the one hand the Teutonic lands outside the Empire—Scandinavia and Northern Germany—form a solid block of Lutheran territory. On the other, the Latin world as a whole remained faithful to Rome, and so also to a great extent did the Germanic provinces within the frontiers of the Empire, such as Flanders, Bavaria and the Austrian provinces. Finally Calvinism, which is the form of Protestantism that appeals most strongly to the Latin mind, has an irregular distribution along the frontier line itself. It appears in Scotland and in the Netherlands, in Switzerland and along the Rhine, as well as on the lower Danube in Hungary and Transylvania. It is also well represented in the two Western kingdoms—England and France. The former was mainly Calvinist, with considerable Catholic, and Catholicizing elements. The latter was Catholic with a strong Calvinist minority and a Calvinizing influence represented by the Jansenists. But in each case the dominant religion is strongly national. In England the Church is Protestant, but above all Anglican; in France it is Catholic, but also Gallican.[1]

[1] It may seem an anomaly that Ireland and Poland, the two border lands of Western culture should be strongly Catholic. Both of these peoples, however, found in Catholicism an invaluable ally against the forces that threatened their own national traditions.

It is true that the Reformation, like the Christological heresies of the 5th century, originated as a religious and theological movement, but its historical importance is due less to its religious doctrine than to the social forces that it came to represent. Luther himself, the religious leader of the movement, is intellectually a man of the Middle Ages rather than of the modern world. His ideas were, in the main, those of the men of the 14th century, Ockham and Wycliffe and Hus. He was entirely alien in spirit from the culture of the Italian Renaissance, and even from that of Northern humanists, like More and Erasmus, whom he describes as " the vilest miscreant that ever disgraced the earth." His originality is due not to his intellectual position, but to the force of his emotional life. He embodies the revolt of the awakening German national spirit against every influence that was felt to be foreign or repressive; against asceticism and all that checked the free expression of the natural instincts, against the intellectualism of Aristotle and St. Thomas, against the whole Latin tradition, above all against the Roman curia and its Italian officials which were to him the representatives of Antichrist and the arch-enemies of the German soul. " The Lutheran Reformation," wrote Nietzsche, " in all its length and breadth was the indignation of the simple against something complicated." It was " a spiritual Peasant Revolt."

Consequently Luther's religious work of reformation and simplification amounted to a de-intellectualization of the Catholic tradition. He eliminated the philosophical and Hellenic elements, and accentuated everything that was Semitic and non-intellectual. He took St. Paul without his Hellenism, and St. Augustine without his Platonism.

Nevertheless, the result of this process was not, as one might suppose, a return to the Oriental type of religion. On the contrary, it produced an accentuation of the purely occidental elements in Christianity. Faith was no longer a human participation in the Divine knowledge, but a purely non-rational experience—the conviction of personal salvation.

The Divine was no longer conceived as pure intelligence—" luce intelletual piena d'amore "—the principle of the intelligibility of the created universe. It was regarded as a despotic power whose decrees predestined man to eternal misery or eternal bliss by the mere *fiat* of arbitrary will. It may seem that this denial of the possibility of human merit, and the insistence on the doctrine of predestination would lead to moral apathy and fatalism. This, however, was not the case. Protestantism was essentially a religion of action. By its hostility to monasticism and asceticism, it destroyed the contemplative ideal and substituted the standard of practical moral duty.[1] And it is this new attitude to secular life—this " Weltbejahung," or World affirmation—that Ritschl and so many other modern Protestants regard as the greatest and most characteristic achievement of the whole movement.

On the other hand, the 19th century view which regarded the Reformation as the starting point of

[1] Thus Luther writes of the St. Bonaventure and the mystics. " They talk much of the union of the will and the understanding, but 'tis all idle fantasy. The right practical divinity is this: Believe in Christ, and do thy duty in that state of life to which God has called thee. In like manner the *Mystical Divinity of Dionysius* is a mere fable and lie. With Plato he chatters: *omnia sunt non ens, et omnia sunt ens;* and so leaves things hanging." *Table Talk* tr. Hazlitt I vii.

modern progress is based on a misconception.[1] The idea of progress only appears in early Protestantism in the old apocalyptic form of a supernatural millenniarism, and that mainly among the proscribed sects, such as the Anabaptists. The seeds of the modern conception of Progress are to be found rather in the Renaissance culture of Catholic Europe. Even Harnack admits that the Catholicism of the Counter Reformation was in closer touch with the new age than Protestantism, except in its purely humanist, i.e. Socinian, form. The former, he says, " worked in alliance with the cultural influences of the period; and poets, humanists, men of learning, discoverers, kings and statesmen soon felt where their proper place was, if," he adds, " they were nothing else than scholars and statesmen."[2]

The Renaissance culture of Southern Europe, however, resembled that of the Protestant Reformation in one respect. It also represents a secularization of life—a reaction from the cloister to the world—from the monastic ideal of religious contemplation to the active life of lay society. The supremacy of the Catholic tradition in the purely religious sphere was not challenged, but it no longer dominated the whole culture. Life was regarded not as a pilgrimage towards eternity, but as a fine art in which every opportunity for knowledge and enjoyment was to be cultivated. As the explorers of the age discovered a new world, so the artists and scholars rediscovered nature and humanity.

[1] The subject is fully dealt with by E. Troeltsch in *Protestantism and Progress* (Eng. trans.).
[2] *History of Dogma*, vol. VII, p. 169 (Eng. trans.)

For it is the artist even more than the scholar or the philosopher who is the true representative of the spirit of the new culture. There has never been a period, not even the classical age of Greece, in which the æsthetic point of view was so dominant in every aspect of life. Even a political realist like Macchiavelli appraises the career of Cæsar Borgia, as though he were criticizing a work of art. The word virtue has lost its moral connotation, and is applied alike to the technical mastery of the artist and the statesman. This æsthetic attitude to life gave a powerful impulse to the study of nature. The art of the Renaissance was an art of observation and experiment, and it had a direct influence on the development of the study of anatomy and perspective. Thus it was the greatest of the artists of the 15th century artists—Leonardo da Vinci—who first realized the possibilities of modern science—not the abstract speculative knowledge which was the Hellenic scientific ideal, but a new science of experiment and applied knowledge which would give man the complete mastery over nature.

" Mechanics," he says, " are the paradise of the mathematical sciences, for in them the fruits of the latter are reaped." " Therefore, O students, study mathematics, and do not build without a foundation." " Experiment is the true interpreter between nature and man." " Experience is never at fault." " Thou, O God, dost sell us all things at the price of labour."

But this new science is not the result of a process of purely inductive reasoning from the data of experience as Bacon and the positivists imagined. It has been truly said by Professor Whitehead that induction itself rests on metaphysics, and the very possibility of science is dependent in that faith in the ultimate rationality of the universe, which the modern world inherited from mediæval scholasticism. It is true that the thinkers of the Renaissance were in revolt against scholasticism and Aristotelianism, but they were far from rejecting metaphysics. On the contrary they had gone back to the more uncompromising intellectualism of the Platonist tradition. The Pythagorean idea of the world as an intelligible order based on number, a mathematical harmony, dominated the whole scientific development of the 16th century and exercised a decisive influence on the rise of the new physics and cosmology. It is common to Copernicus, Galileo and Kepler. The Timaeus which a modern writer has described as " a picture of the depth to which natural science can be degraded by a great mind"[1] was regarded by these men as a key to the mystery of the universe, and from it they derived their belief in the mathematical structure of reality which was both the intellectual foundation and the imaginative inspiration of their whole work. Thus modern science owes its birth to the union of the creative genius of the Renaissance art with the mathematical idealism of Platonic metaphysics. And this romantic marriage was the source not only of a new physical synthesis, but of the vast material and economic progress of the modern world. As Henri Poincaré has said: " We have only to open our eyes to see that the conquests of industry which have enriched so many practical men would never have seen the day if these practical men had been the only ones to exist, and if they had not been preceded by disinterested

[1] Dr. Singer in *Religion and Science*, 1927, p. 20.

madmen who died poor, who never thought of the useful, but who were nevertheless guided by something more than their own caprice."[1]

But while the new synthesis was infinitely superior to that of the 13th century on its physical side, it was inferior in that it no longer embraced the whole of reality. Not only had man lost his central place in the universe as the link between the higher reality of spirit and the lower reality of matter, he was in danger of being pushed outside the intelligible order altogether. For if the universe is conceived as a closed mechanical order governed by mathematical laws, there is no longer any room in it for the moral and spiritual values which had hitherto been regarded as the supreme reality. It would seem to follow that the world of human consciousness was subjective and unreal, and that man himself was nothing but a by-product of the vast mechanical order which the new science had revealed.

It is true that this conclusion was not actually drawn by any but a few eccentric free-thinkers, such as Vanini and Hobbes. The reality of the moral and spiritual order was admitted, not only by the vast majority of men, but by the leaders of the new thought themselves. But it could no longer be integrated with the system of the material universe in a single order of reality. Consequently the most powerful attempt of the new thought to produce a philosophic synthesis —the Cartesian system—resulted in a strict philosophical dualism of mind and spirit, " res extensa and res cogitans." Spirit and matter were two separate worlds which could only be brought into contact

[1] H. Poincaré, *Science et Méthode*, p. 9.

with one another by the intervention of an external power—the Cartesian deity.

And this philosophical dualism corresponds to the cultural dualism which was so marked a feature of the age. There was no longer, as in the Middle Ages, a single tradition of culture which united every aspect of life in the service of a common doctrine and a common ideal. The secular culture of the Renaissance and the religious tradition of the Reformation and the Counter-Reformation failed to coalesce with one another. In Southern Europe, it is true, the Catholic revival was able to incorporate or at least to use for its own purposes the art and music of the new age, but it failed to assimilate the new movement of scientific thought. The religious and the scientific traditions remained apart from one another, and each hampered the other in the attainment of its full development.

And in Northern Europe this dualism of culture was even more pronounced. The culture of the Renaissance and that of the Reformation were two separate worlds, entirely alien from one another in spirit and without any common ground on which they could meet. In England, the tradition of the Reformation was reaching its climax in the Puritan movement at the same time that the Renaissance culture was producing a diametrically opposite conception of life in the Shakespearian drama. And in Holland the orthodox Calvinism that dominated the country was bitterly hostile to the great Dutch humanists such as Grotius and Vondel and Huyghens. The men who sought to reconcile religion and science in an intellectual synthesis were exiles and solitaries, like Descartes and Spinoza.

Moreover, it is easy to exaggerate the influence of the new ideas. Society as a whole remained as completely dominated by religious ideas as it had been during the Middle Ages. Indeed it may be doubted whether religion has ever excited a more passionate interest in men's minds than during the century that lies between the years 1560 and 1660, the age of the Puritans and the Jansenists, of Bœhme and Crashaw, of St. Teresa and St. Vincent de Paul. Alike in politics, in literature and in private life, religious interests were everywhere the predominant ones, and coloured the whole mentality of the age. Unlike the religion of the Middle Ages, however, that of the Post-Reformation period was a source of division and strife rather than the principle of social unity. The intensity of religious convictions served only to increase the bitterness of social strife, and a century of religious warfare left Europe farther from unity than ever. Christendom was sinking into a chaos of warring sects, each of which claimed to be the sole representative of the Christian tradition. The imposing unity of the French monarchy of Louis XIV was only purchased at the expense of the expulsion of the Huguenots, and the alienation of the Jansenists. And if religious unification was difficult in France, in England it had become a sheer impossibility. In the course of less than fifty years (1640–1690) the Government had been successively Presbyterian, Independent, Anglican and Catholic, and none of these had proved strong enough to suppress or eliminate its rivals.

Just as the French religious wars of the 16th century had given rise to the party of Politiques, who placed national unity before all religious considerations, so,

187

too, the religious struggle in England had caused statesmen to realize that the only hope of peace and order lay in the establishment of some form of mutual toleration. This is the real meaning of the Revolution Settlement and the cause of its wide significance in the history of European culture. It is true that the Revolution of 1688 was apparently a defeat for the principle of Toleration since it was directed against the Declaration of Indulgence, and demanded the reinforcement of the Test Act and the Penal Laws. Actually, however, it marks the end of the attempt to base society on a religious foundation, and the beginning of the progressive secularization of the English state. According to John Locke, the philosopher of the Revolutionary Settlement, the prime duty of a Government is not to defend the Christian faith but to secure the rights of private property, " for the sake of which men enter into society." Thus, as Lord Acton says, the English Revolution substituted " for the Divine Right of Kings the divine right of Freeholders." For two centuries and more England was to be the Paradise of the Man of Property.

This tendency towards the secularization of the state was but one aspect of a wider movement which was making for the secularization of European culture. The peace of Westphalia in 1648 had set a final seal on the religious divisions of Europe, and it was becoming increasingly obvious that it was impossible to restore the spiritual unity of Christendom by war and diplomacy. Nevertheless Western civilization remained from many points of view a unity. The development of the literary culture of the Renaissance and still more of the new scientific knowledge was not limited by national and religious boundaries. Protestants like Kepler and Leibnitz and Newton co-operated with Catholics like Copernicus and Descartes and Galileo to build up the edifice of modern science. Thus the international character of the new learning prevented what might otherwise have occurred—the separation of Western Europe into two distinct self-contained cultures, respectively Catholic and Protestant, while on the other hand it afforded a basis for the reconstitution of the spiritual unity of the European culture. There was an increasing tendency among the intellectuals to turn away from religious controversy and to fall back on the idea of a rational religion common to all sensible men. This tendency was already making itself felt in 16th century France as we see from Montaigne and Charron, and in the following century it found more explicit expression in England with Lord Herbert of Cherbury, Chillingworth and Locke. Finally, in the 18th century it attained its full development with the English Deists and their disciples the French philosophers, who attempted to substitute the Religion of Nature for orthodox Christianity as the ruling faith of modern civilization.

The new creed finds a classical expression in Pope's Essay on Man and his Universal Prayer, and it is easy to understand how a generation that was wearied with the endless subtleties of the Jansenist or the Arminian controversy could turn with relief to the triumphant commonplaces that flow so easily in Pope's limpid Augustan couplets. And the same ideas reached an even wider public when served up with the salt of Voltaire's wit.

But in spite of its unorthodox and even anti-Christian character, all the positive elements in the new creed were derived from the old religious tradition of Christendom. For a civilization cannot strip itself of its past in the same way that a philosopher discards a theory. The religion that has governed the life of a people for a thousand years enters into its very being, and moulds all its thought and feeling. When the philosophers of the 18th century attempted to substitute their new rationalist doctrines for the ancient faith of Christendom, they were in reality simply abstracting from it those elements which had entered so deeply into their own thought that they no longer recognized their origin. Eighteenth century Deism was but the ghost or shadow of Christianity, a mental abstraction from the reality of a historical religion, which possessed no independent life of its own. It retained certain fundamental Christian conceptions— the belief in a beneficent Creator, the idea of an overruling Providence which ordered all things for the best, and the chief precepts of the Christian moral law, but all these were desupernaturalized and fitted into the utilitarian rational scheme of contemporary philosophy. Thus the moral law was divested of all ascetic and other-worldly elements and assimilated to practical philanthropy, and the order of Providence was transformed into a mechanistic natural law. Above all this was the case with the idea of Progress, for while the new philosophy had no place for the supernaturalism of the Christian eschatology, it could not divest itself of the Christian teleological conception of life. Thus the belief in the moral perfectibility and the indefinite progress of the human race took the place of the Christian faith in the life of the world to come, as the final goal of human effort. This idea lies at the root of the whole philosophic movement, and it was fully formulated long before the days of the Encyclopædist propaganda. And it is quite in accordance with what I have said regarding the origins of this circle of ideas, that its author should have been a priest—the first of that long line of sceptical and reforming clerics, such as Mably, Condillac, Morelly, Raynal and Sieyès, who were so characteristic of the Age of Enlightenment.

The Abbé de St. Pierre was a prophet who received little honour in his own country. He had the reputation of a crank and a bore. It was for his statue that Voltaire wrote the lines:

> "Ce n'est là qu'un portrait.
> L'original dirait quelque sottise."

Yet his fertile brain originated most of the projects that were to be realized or attempted by the Liberals of the next two centuries—international arbitration and the abolition of war, free education and the reform of female education, the establishment of a poor rate and the abolition of pauperism, not to mention other inventions peculiar to himself, such as the social utilization of sermons. But underlying all this was his fundamental doctrine of the " perpetual and unlimited augmentation of the universal human reason," which will inevitably produce the golden age and the establishment of paradise on earth. Nor would this happy consummation be long delayed. All that was necessary was the conversion of the powers that be to the Abbé's principles, for St. Pierre shared the beliefs of his age as to the unlimited possibilities of governmental action.

o   191

And this doctrine became the ruling conception of the new age, for while the God of the Deists was but a pale abstraction, a mere *deus ex machina*, the belief in Progress was an ideal capable of stirring men's emotions and arousing a genuine religious enthusiasm. Nor was it limited to the followers of the French philosophic rationalism. It played an equally important part in the formation of German Idealism and English Utilitarian Liberalism. In England, its derivation from theological presuppositions is particularly clear. Its chief exponents, Price and Priestley, were Nonconformist ministers, and the earlier theorists of progress in Great Britain, Turnbull, and above all David Hartley, rested their whole argument on a theological basis. The turbid flood of English Puritanism had spread, in the 18th century, into the wide and shallow waters of Liberal Protestantism, and the visionary millenniarist ideas of the earlier period had been transformed into a rational enthusiasm for moral and material progress. Even the economic doctrines of Adam Smith rest on a foundation of religious optimism, which remained a characteristic feature of later British Liberalism.

At first sight the contemporary movement in France is the diametrical opposite of this, since it was marked by a bitter hostility to Christianity. But we must not be misled by the anti-religious diatribes of the French philosophers. Real scepticism is usually tolerant, and the intolerance and iconoclasm of the 18th century philosophers, like that of the 16th century Reformers, was the fanaticism of the sectaries of a new gospel. The French Enlightenment was, in fact, the last of the great European heresies, and its appeal to Reason was in itself an act of faith which admitted of no criticism. Even materialists, like Helvetius and Holbach, shared the Deist belief in the transcendence of Reason and the inevitability of intellectual and moral progress, though there was nothing in their premisses to warrant such assumptions.

Moreover the movement of philosophic rationalism was only one side of the French 18th century development. No less important was the social idealism of Rousseau, which was far more pronouncedly religious in spirit. Rousseau was at once a revolutionary and a reactionary of the type of Tolstoi. He turned away from modern civilization and the creed of scientific progress towards the simplicity of an idealized state of nature, and though he believed no less intensely than Diderot or Condorcet in the perfectibility of man and society, he looked for its realization, not to Reason and external organization, but to the inner light of conscience, and to obedience to the eternal laws of nature that are written in the human heart.

It is true that his religion was not that of orthodox Protestantism. Reduced to an intellectual statement, it differed hardly at all from that of Diderot and Voltaire; it was the spirit behind that was different. All the vehemence of religious conviction with which his Calvinist ancestors had affirmed the doctrine of Original Sin and the impotence of the human will was turned by Rousseau to the service of the diametrically opposite doctrines of the original goodness of human nature and the perfectibility of society, and so, too, he attacked the actual state as the one cause of all man's evils and sufferings with the same violence that the Calvinists had shown towards the

Catholic Church of their time. And indeed the work of Rousseau was a new Reformation, which aroused no less enthusiasm and fanaticism in the minds of his followers, and was no less destructive in its practical effects than that of the 16th century. The neurotic unpractical dreamer of Les Charmettes and Montmorency kindled a fire which destroyed the state and society of the Ancien Régime, and utterly changed the face of Europe.

It is true that Rousseau's ideas regarding the perfection of the state of Nature and the corrupting influences of civilization seem at first sight hardly reconcilable with the belief in Progress. But it was the optimistic side of his doctrine—his faith in human nature and in the perfectibility of society—which made the deepest impression on his contemporaries. The work of the earlier philosophic movement had already destroyed the spiritual foundations of the post-Reformation society and had prepared men's minds for the coming of a new order; its actual realization was due to the influence of Rousseau which supplied the necessary dynamic of religious conviction and enthusiasm.

This is the real source of the revolutionary movement on the continent. Social and political revolution has become so common a feature of modern European life that we are apt to forget how rare such movements are in history. They occur only when a culture is undergoing a process of internal transformation. Social revolution is an index of spiritual change.

Thus the French Revolution was not so much a revolt against misgovernment and oppression, as an attempt to restore the unity of European society on the foundation of the new ideas. Not only in France, but in every country of Europe where the influence of Rousseau had penetrated, it aroused a sympathetic response.

Wordsworth has described the wonderful atmosphere of those years when it was a joy to be alive:

> Europe at that time was thrilled with joy
> France standing on the top of golden hours
> And human nature seeming born again

For the revolutionaries did not limit themselves to political reforms, such as the establishment of a new constitution and a new legal code, they aspired to refashion society from its foundations. The new calendar of the revolutionary era symbolizes the complete break that was made with the past, and the belief that a new age had begun for humanity. The doctrines of Rousseau were the dogmas of the new state, and were surrounded by the ritual of an official cult in the feasts of the revolutionary calendar culminating in Robespierre's solemn celebration of the Feast of the Supreme Being. But the victory of the new ideals ended swiftly in failure and disillusionment. The atrocities of the Reign of Terror were a grim commentary on the extravagant optimism of the 18th century reformers and the belief of Rousseau in the essential goodness of human nature. The great apostle of the idea of Progress, Condorcet, was himself a victim of the Terror, and the place of the generous idealists and reformers who had presided over the early stages of the Revolution was taken by self-seeking and corrupt politicians like Barras and Rewbell.

Thus it is not surprising that the disappointment of the boundless hopes that had accompanied the Revolution produced a reaction against the whole current of 18th century thought. While the Revolution had seemed to the men of 1789 the justification of their belief in the perfectibility of the human race, after the Reign of Terror it appeared as a blind force of destruction that threatened the existence of European civilization. The failure of the revolutionary persecution of the Church made men realize that the historic faith of Christendom was far too deeply rooted to be replaced by the hollow abstractions of the Theophilanthropists and the Decadary Cult, and writers like Burke in England and de Maistre and Chateaubriand in France turned to the Christian religion as the one power that was capable of saving society. Thus they returned to the earlier tradition that had given European culture its unity, and appealed to the ideal of mediæval Christendom against its secularized 18th century derivative. This, however, involved the abandonment of the idea of Progress, and a fundamental criticism of the principles of the 18th century philosophic movement.

Henceforth European society—at least on the Continent—was divided in two camps, on the one side the adherents of the Liberal revolutionary principles, on the other the followers of the Catholic and Conservative tradition.

Yet the Revolution itself was, as we have seen, the result of ideas which had their root in the Christian tradition, and this has been fully recognised by many of its historians, such as Buchez and Lamartine. For instance, the latter writes in his history of the Girondins : " The Revolution had been prepared by a century of philosophy, which was apparently sceptical but really believing. The scepticism of the 18th century only extended to the external forms and the supernatural dogmas of Christianity; it passionately adopted its moral teaching and its social intention."

It is, however, necessary to make a distinction between the rationalist Liberalism of the Enlightenment, on the one hand, and the revolutionary idealism of Rousseau and his followers on the other. They are both dependent on an anterior religious ideal, which they have transposed or interpreted in a purely social sense, but each of them represents a different religious tradition. The older philosophic theory of Progress, with its dogmatic appeal to Reason, and its reliance on the authority of an enlightened despotism, corresponds to the Christian tradition in its orthodox form, while the doctrine of the revolutionary idealists has an even closer affinity with the apocalyptic hopes of the earlier Millenniarists and Anabaptists. Indeed it is often difficult to distinguish the descriptions of the social millennium of the revolutionaries from those of a purely religious apocalyptic. "In that blessed day," writes Godwin, the leading English representative of revolutionary idealism, "there will be no war, no crimes, no administration of justice, as it is called, and no government. Besides this, there will be neither disease, anguish, melancholy, nor resentment. Every man will seek with ineffable ardour the good of all. Mind will be active and eager, and yet never disappointed."[1]

So, too, Godwin's son-in-law and disciple, Shelley, in spite of his worship of Hellenic antiquity, unconsciously derived his ideals from the religious tradition

[1] W. Godwin, *Inquiry Concerning Political Justice*, II, 528.

which he so bitterly attacked. What could be more Christian than the whole idea of " Prometheus Unbound," the salvation of humanity by the suffering and love of an innocent victim? And in the same way, Shelley's ideal of liberty is utterly foreign to the tradition of Hellenism. It is nothing less than " the glorious liberty of the children of God," for which the whole creation groans, and the effects of which overflow from humanity to the external world and transform the whole order of nature.

This millenniarist conception of Progress is specially characteristic of the early Socialists. It reached its climax in Fourier, whose speculations surpass in extravagance the wildest dreams of Cerinthus and his followers. For according to Fourier all the present evils of the material world are bound up with our defective social arrangements. Nature is bad, because man is bad. As soon as the new social order of the Fourierist gospel is introduced, the earth will be transformed. The waters of the ocean will change to lemonade, and the useless and ugly marine monsters, which are the images of our own passions, will be replaced by useful and agreeable creatures. Human life will be extended to three or four centuries, and there will be thirty-seven million poets equal to Homer, and thirty-seven million philosophers like Newton.

In comparison with Fourier, Robert Owen and the St. Simonians appear mere cautious rationalists, but nevertheless millenniarist ideals colour all their thought and were transmitted by them to the later political socialism. The driving force of the Socialist movement, in fact, has always been its belief in a social apocalypse.

But while the origin of Socialism is primarily due to the economic interpretation of the revolutionary idealism of Rousseau, it also owed much to the influence of German thought. Now in Germany the theory of Progress had developed on different lines from those that it followed in France, its original home. The German philosophers did not share the open hostility to Christianity that marked the French Enlightenment, indeed some of them were deeply influenced by the mystical ideas of German Pietism. Moreover, they had a much wider and deeper appreciation of history than their French predecessors. Instead of emphasizing the contradiction between the Age of Reason and the Age of Faith, they brought Christianity and historical religion into their scheme of progress. Thus Lessing, in his famous pamphlet on " The Education of the Human Race," bases his philosophy of history on a progressive religious revelation, which he assimilates to the doctrine of Tertullian and Joachim of Flora concerning the three world ages of the Christian dispensation.

The Third Age of the Reign of the Spirit and the Eternal Gospel was conceived by Lessing as the Age of Reason and of the self-realization of humanity, but it was the fulfilment, not the contradiction, of the Christian revelation. The influence of Lessing's theory was extraordinarily deep and far reaching. It lies at the root of the development of Liberal or Modernist Protestantism in Germany, it affected the St. Simonian socialists in France,[1] and even Comte's famous Law of the Three Stages was probably

---

[1] *The Education of the Human Race* was translated by E. Rodriguez, the St. Simonian, when Comte was still a member of the group.

199

influenced by it. Above all it was adopted with enthusiasm by all the great German idealist philosophers, each of whom interpreted it according to the requirements of his own system.

It finds full expression in Fichte's theory of the Five Ages of Humanity through which the collective life of the race moves to its appointed end. For the Fifth Age in which Humanity attains its full stature as a free and living image of the Eternal Reason is, he says, none other than the Millennial Kingdom of the Apocalypse: the reign of the Spirit. But it is in the philosophy of Schelling that this religious interpretation of the idea of Progress reaches its climax. The theories of this Prussian professor find a closer parallel in the thought of mediæval mystics, like Erigena and Eckhart, than in that of the philosophers of the Enlightenment. The idea of Progress has entirely lost its rational and utilitarian connotation and has become simply the human aspect of the eternal movement of return by which the created world is brought back into God.

This mystical conception of progress colours the thought of the Romantic period in Germany, and finds expression in the writings of Frederick Schlegel, K. C. Krause and many others. In the case of Hegel, on the other hand, the attitude to history is far more realist, and he is concerned rather with the philosophical justification of the actual than with mystical speculations regarding the future of humanity. The Spirit finds its embodiment not in the New Jerusalem but in the Prussian State. Nevertheless, the Hegelian conception of history remains fundamentally religious. It is a philosophy of Incarnation, of the progressive self-manifestation of God in history. And though the conception has been robbed of its supernatural elements and covered with a veneer of rationalism, its theological ancestry is obvious enough.[1]

Thus the philosophy of Hegel is an important link and channel of influence between the mystical idealism of the romantic thinkers and the rationalism and positivism of the later 19th century thought. For while the Hegelianism of the Right was in intimate relations with the mystical transcendentalism of Schelling, the Hegelianism of the Left led on to Feuerbach's religious subjectivism, and even to the historical materialism of Karl Marx.

In the first half of the 19th century the Idea of Progress had attained its full development. It dominated the three main currents of European thought, Rationalist Liberalism, Revolutionary Socialism and Transcendental Idealism. It evoked all the enthusiasm and faith of a genuine religion. Indeed it seemed to many that the dream of St. Simon was on the eve of its fulfilment, and that " the New Christianity," the Religion of Progress, was to restore to Europe the spiritual unity which she had lost since the Middle Ages. Actually, however, the course of European development in the following period failed to realize these ideals. The 19th century was " the Century of Hope " but it was also the Century of Disillusion.

[1] For example the mystical theory of the Three World Ages—of the Father, the Son and the Holy Spirit—a theory which had once more been put into current circulation by Lessing, plays a considerable part in Hegel's thought. Indeed it is not improbable that the fundamental Hegelian doctrine of the triple dialectic in its application to history and life was inspired from this quarter.

·IX

THE AGE OF SCIENCE AND INDUSTRIALISM
THE DECLINE OF THE RELIGION OF PROGRESS

I

THE current of philosophic enlightenment and political revolution which was described in the last
chapter represents only one side of the great movement of change which has affected Europe and the
world in the last two centuries. At the same time
that the influence of the new ideas was producing an
intellectual and political revolution on the continent,
in England the material conditions of civilization
were being transformed by the new economic methods
which produced the Industrial Revolution.

The two movements were the result of common
or parallel forces. Both of them had their origin in
the new world-view of the English Revolutionary
period—the age of Newton and Locke. Both of them
were equally indebted to the new science of nature
and to the old religious tradition, in its secularized
Deist form. Nevertheless the common principles of
the new movement were not strong enough to eliminate
the underlying differences of national character and
religious tradition which separated Protestant England

from Catholic France. In the latter country the leaders of the movement of the Enlightenment showed none of the cautious realism which characterized the English thinkers. They attempted to replace the unity of Catholicism by a no less universal philosophic orthodoxy, to substitute the reign of science and reason for that of theology and faith.

In England, on the other hand, there was no violent breach with religion, for the prevailing spirit of the Latitudinarian Whig divines was so similar to that of their Deist opponents that there was little room for fundamental disagreement. Thus in England and Scotland there was developed a kind of *via media* between traditional Christianity and the new ideas which was represented by orthodox divines, such as Paley and Turnbull, as well as by Unitarians, such as Priestley and Price, and laymen, such as David Hartley and Adam Smith. All these were apostles of the idea of Progress, and to them is due that combination of individualism with strict moral discipline, and of religious optimism with an enthusiasm for social and political reform which was to inspire the age of the Industrial Revolution and the beginnings of English Liberalism. Hence at the same time that the French were attempting to reconstruct society on abstract principles, the English were devoting themselves to a practical utilitarian activity which was to have an even greater effect on the future of civilization. For it was the enterprise and industry of 18th century Britain that first realized the dream of the Renaissance scientists, and brought the forces of nature under human control by scientific means. The Industrial Revolution was the fruit of the mathematical achievements of Galileo and Newton which had laid the foundations of the modern science of mechanics, and the mechanical civilization of the industrial age was the practical corollary of the mechanical order of nature revealed by the Newtonian physics.

Nevertheless the material potentialities of the new science might have waited in vain for their fulfilment, as was the case with Greek mechanics in the ancient world, had it not been for the social initiative of British industry. This initiative received its moral impetus from the religious traditions of English society. Historians like Troeltsch and Max Weber have shown how much the industrial movement owes to the moral and social ideals of Puritanism. The Protestant as-ceticism of the 17th and 18th centuries did not lead men to fly from the world and to give up all their goods to the poor and the Church, as in the Middle Ages. It inculcated the duty of unremitting industry and thrift, while at the same time it discouraged rigorously every kind of self-indulgence and extrava-gance in the expenditure of what had been gained. Thus there grew up a new social type, the hard-working, conscientious, abstemious man of business, whose only interests were in his counting-house and in the meeting-house of his sect; men who spared themselves no more than their employees, and who looked on their work as a kind of religious vocation.

It was men of this stamp who supplied the driving power of the Industrial Revolution, and were the founders of the economic power of Britain and the United States. It is, indeed, difficult to realize the importance of this element in English culture, owing to the comparatively small part that it took in the literary and political life of the age. The sectarian tradition existed as a kind of underworld quite apart from the dominant aristocratic culture of Pope and Bolingbroke, of Horace Walpole and Fox, of Hume and Gibbon. Nevertheless, it had a far greater influence than the latter on the rise of the new economic order. Nor was its influence limited to the economic field, for many of the philosophers and scientists themselves belonged to this nonconformist culture. The leaders of scientific thought were found not at the great universities, nor, as in France, in the centre of fashionable society; they were the sons of north country weavers and blacksmiths who combined an intense sectarian religiosity with their devotion to the new knowledge. Priestley was a Unitarian minister, Dalton a Quaker schoolmaster, Faraday a Sandemanian elder.

Certainly such men were rare, and the average leader of the industrial movement was far from being a disinterested idealist, but the narrow and intense spirit of Puritanism permeated the whole movement and gave English middle-class society the moral force to carry out the vast material labour of the Industrial Revolution. Consequently the real spirit of the age is to be found not in the somewhat arid eudæmonism of utilitarian ethics, but in a sombre asceticism which sacrificed all the pleasures and graces of life to the ideals of moral duty and economic power.

In theory the new development was the result of the application of the Liberal doctrines of Free Trade and *Laissez Faire*. In reality it was due to a vast co-operative effort towards the economic conquest of the world which involved a very high degree of social discipline and organization. The true note of the age was not economic freedom, but economic conquest and exploitation.

The whole process may be compared to the conquest and unification of the ancient world by Rome in the first and second centuries B.C. It is true that the Roman imperial movement was essentially military, and the economic aspects of it were secondary, whereas the modern world organization is primarily economic, and the military factor has been subordinate. Nevertheless the builders of the Roman roads were doing the same work as the English engineers who planned the first railways, and the Roman publicans and financiers played somewhat the same part in the expansion of the Empire as the European capitalists and bond holders of modern times. But the advance of modern Western civilization has been on a vaster scale, and involves wider issues. The revolution in the means of transport and production has opened the whole world to the economic exploitation of the organized industrial and financial power of the West. Regions of which the very existence was unknown a century ago are to-day producing wealth for the European markets and are in closer communication with Europe than England had been with the Continent in the 18th century. In America great modern cities with millions of inhabitants have grown up in the prairies and forests where, a century before, savage tribes were still leading the life of the hunters of the Stone Age. Even the great oriental civilizations, whose tradition of culture is far older than our own and which have remained for ages as closed worlds, have been drawn into the net of the new industrial scientific culture. Everywhere the old independent standards of life and the old self-sufficient agrarian economy have broken down, and the world has become a single community, with an international economic life and common ideals of material civilization.

Thus modern Europe and America appear as the heirs and continuators of the old Roman tradition of world pacification and organization on a far wider stage than that of the Mediterranean world. But the new Western hegemony is not, like the old, a purely material conquest, based on naked military force. Its advance has gone hand in hand with the spread of liberal ideas and of political democracy. The 19th century was an age of political reform and humanitarian idealism. It has witnessed all over the world the destruction of slavery, the abolition of torture and cruel penal codes and a systematic attempt to combat famine and disease. It is true that modern " progress and enlightenment " have often proved more fatal to the survival of primitive peoples than the Roman sword, but that was not the intention of their disseminators, who believed that nothing but good could result from the substitution of Manchester goods and hymn books for nakedness and cannibalism. And the disappearance of a few tribes of savages must have appeared, after all, a small thing in comparison with the vast increase of wealth and population which resulted from the opening up of new continents and oceans.

We cannot wonder at the optimism of the Victorians and their contemporaries, the continental Liberals, since the amazing social and material changes that they witnessed seemed to afford a tangible proof of the theory of progress, and to mark the beginning of a new era in the history of humanity. Nevertheless, these hopes have not been fulfilled, and the last fifty years have seen a sharp reaction from the triumphant optimism of the earlier period.

Material progress, unrestricted competition, and national rivalries have led to a social crisis which threatens not only the prosperity, but the very existence of European civilization. The capitalist organization of industry has led, no less than military conquest, to the exploitation of subject classes and nationalities. It is true that the worst results of modern industrialism cannot be compared with the horrors of the Roman slave system, but the existence of the modern ideals of humanity and liberty has caused the evils of the modern system to be far more strongly felt. And it must be admitted that the industrial movement, while raising the general standard of life, has caused a retrogression in the position of the ordinary worker. Politically he gained full rights of citizenship such as he never possessed at any other period of the world's history; economically he lost the control that the craftsman possessed under the old system of hand industry over the conditions of his work, and became a mere cog in the vast machinery of modern industrialism.

Under such circumstances it was inevitable that the earlier revolutionary propaganda on behalf of the Rights of Man should ultimately take an economic form. Socialism was, in fact, as we have seen, the heir of the earlier revolutionary Liberalism. In spite of the scientific interpretation that it received at the hands of Karl Marx and his disciples, it was like the doctrine of Rousseau no cold rational theory, but a creed and a religion.

The Marxian interpretation of history and social evolution must be judged as an economic, or rather philosophic, theory; but considered as a sociological phenomenon, the revolutionary socialism of modern Europe must be classed with the obscure movements of revolt that shook the ancient world in the first and second centuries B.C. It marks the failure of the great movement of material progress and organization to satisfy the instincts of the human element, on whose labour the social edifice rests. It is not merely a dissatisfaction with material conditions, it is a movement of spiritual disaffection against the modern social order and a demand for a new life.

But it is not only the Socialists and the revolutionaries who threaten the modern European order. As in the case of the militarist capitalism of the later Roman Republic, the greatest danger to the industrialist capitalism of modern Europe comes from its own inherent instability. The exploitation of the world by the new industrialized societies of Western Europe, like that of the Mediterranean lands by Rome in the first and second centuries B.C., has been too rapid to continue indefinitely. The prosperity of the industrialized societies of the nineteenth century rested on a temporary monopoly of the new methods—on a limited output combined with a continually expanding world market.

But to-day these factors are reversed. The new methods are becoming common to the whole world, and the old monopoly enjoyed by the leading industrial Powers of Western Europe is rapidly disappearing. Every nation—even those of the Far East, like Japan

—is organizing itself to take its share in the world markets, while at the same time restricting those markets by a rigorous protective tariff.

Nowhere has the influence of these new conditions been felt more strongly than in England, the classical home of the old industry. At the present moment we see its effects not only in the crisis of the coal industry, but in the disastrous state of all the so-called " heavy industries " subsisting by the foreign market, which has resulted in the work of a dustman being often better paid than that of a skilled engineer. Moreover, during the period of Free Trade and open markets the industrial population increased far beyond the limits of the national agricultural capacity, so that England is almost entirely dependent on an imported food supply, which must be financed by the industrial export, in the face of growing competition abroad and prohibitive duties.

Thus the vast and rapid development of the new economic order has produced a serious reaction, and Europe's position of world leadership seems threatened less than a century after its attainment. For if the organization of the world by Europe was in the main due to her economic supremacy, the passing of that supremacy would seem to portend the breakdown of her international leadership. Already the East is reacting against the supremacy of the West, and claiming an equality of position; and the internal power of resistance of European civilization is weakened alike by national rivalry and disunion, and by the social discontent of international labour.

But the roots of the instability of our civilization go even deeper than this. The economic and social changes of the last century have produced a revolution in the relations of man to nature and in the vital structure of society itself. They have destroyed the biological equilibrium between human society and its natural environment. Hitherto in every European society the higher urban civilization has been a comparatively light superstructure which rested on the broad and solid foundation of rural society. Whatever were the intellectual changes and the political transformation of the ruling and self-conscious social classes, the life of the peasant went on unchanged, following the unvarying rhythm of the life of nature and the changes of the seasons. In many parts of Europe this peasant life was sufficiently differentiated to possess a distinct art and culture of its own, but even in England, where this was not the case, the countryfolk possessed their own traditions and their own way of life which were but little affected by the contemporary standards of the educated classes.

Thus there existed in every society, as it were a vital reservoir of human material, from which the culturally active elements of the cities and the ruling classes could derive new life and energy. There was a continual movement of population from the country to the towns, and from the lower to the upper strata of society, which served to replace the human material that had been exhausted by the strain of an artificial way of life and an intenser form of social activity. We have only to look at the pedigrees of a few representative English county families or men of business to realize how extensive was this movement of social circulation, and how the ruling elements in society were constantly brought into contact with the instinctive vitality of the peasant substratum.

To-day all this is changed. In highly industrialized societies like Great Britain, the country folk form a small minority in a predominantly urban population, and are themselves rapidly becoming urbanized in their standards of culture and their view of life. Even in the countries where agriculture retains its economic importance, the peasant no longer preserves his separate way of life, and all the powers of the state and of public opinion, acting through politics and the press, standardized education and universal military service, co-operate to produce a population of completely uniform habits and education. Modern urban civilization no longer has any contact with the soil or the instinctive life of nature. The whole population lives in a high state of nervous tension, even where it has not reached the frenzied activity of American city life. Everywhere the conditions of life are becoming more and more artificial, and make an increasing demand on men's nervous energies. The rhythm of social life is accelerated, since it is no longer forced to keep time with the life of nature. This complete revolution in the conditions of life must inevitably have a profound effect upon the future of mankind. For it is not merely a transformation of material culture, it involves a biological change which must affect the character of the race itself.

It is as yet impossible to know if man will be able to adapt himself successfully to conditions which are so entirely different from those of the past. There is a danger that the sudden outburst of energy which has characterized the new urban-industrial civilization may be followed by a premature exhaustion of social and physical vitality, and may thus become a cause of social degeneration. Or, on the other hand, it may be possible to reach a new stage of social equilibrium in which the vital forces of society are scientifically safeguarded and preserved from the deteriorating influences of the new conditions.

But even if this is possible, the dangers inherent in the new situation are very threatening. We have only to look back to the age of Roman world organization, which in many respects bears so striking a resemblance to our own, in order to see how rapidly the process of urbanization may change the character of a culture and affect its social vitality. Here there was no question of senescence. Society came near to dissolution while at the very height of its cultural activities, when its human types were more vigorous than ever before. The danger to civilization came, not from any lack of vital energy, but from a sudden change of conditions—a material revolution, which broke down the organic constitution of the society.

Rome, more than any other city-state of antiquity, was essentially an agrarian state. The foundation of her power and of her very existence was the peasant-soldier citizen. The lands of the Latin farmers grouped in strategic positions all over Italy, and those of the Roman citizens concentrated in the best land of central Italy, gave the Roman power a broader basis than any other ancient state possessed and profoundly differentiated the Roman legion from the mercenary armies of the Hellenistic states. The peasant religion, the peasant economy, and the peasant morale underlie all the characteristic achievements of the republican epoch.

213

But with the conquest of the Mediterranean all this was changed. A progressive degeneration and transformation of the characteristic Roman types took place. The fundamental peasant-soldier-citizen gave way—as farmer to the slave—as soldier to the professional—as citizen to a vast urban proletariat living on Government doles and the bribes of politicians. So, too, the noble began to give place to the millionaire, and the magistrate to the military adventurer. Rome became more and more a predatory state that lived by war and plunder, and exhausted her own strength with that of her victims. The republic slowly foundered amidst massacres and counter massacres, slave wars and a continual growth of political and financial corruption. It was only by the genius and the persistence of Augustus that Rome regained some hold on her traditions. And even Augustus failed to cure the fundamental malady of the Roman state, though he well realized its importance. He could not restore the citizen farmer in the place of the slave, nor could he cope with the cosmopolitan urban development of the city of Rome itself. For it was literally Rome that killed Rome. The great cosmopolitan city of gold and marble, the successor of Alexandria and Antioch, had nothing in common with the old capital of the rural Latin state. It served no social function, it was an end in itself, and its population drawn from every nation under heaven existed mainly to draw their Government doles, and to attend the free spectacles with which the Government provided them. It was a vast, useless burden on the back of the empire which broke at last under the increasing strain.

It is true that the urban development of our own

age has not the same parasitic character as that of the ancient world. Moreover, the possibilities of scientific control over the material conditions of social life and even over its organic development are infinitely greater. Nevertheless, the social changes with which we have to deal are also far more fundamental and more universal in their consequences. Whatever the possibilities of a new social development may be, they cannot be realized by blind or uncoordinated activity. Our civilization needs social and moral unification even more than did the Roman world in the age of Augustus, since the interests at stake are even greater.

If modern Europe falls either through internal revolution or through loss of her world leadership, modern civilization falls with her. For that civilization was entirely a European creation, and there is no force outside Europe to-day capable of carrying on her work, whatever be the case a century or two hence. Either the incipient world order that has been the work of the last century of Western progress will break down and disappear, or it must be completed by a further process of stabilization and organization which will make possible an age of true world civilization under Western leadership.

At the present hour any such policy of social reorganization seems outside the range of practical politics. If we look to the Right, the parties of order and loyalty to the traditions of the past are just those which are most firmly wedded to national particularism and strife, and most bound by vested interests in economic matters. On the other hand, the parties of the Left who profess the highest ideals of social justice and international brotherhood care little for the historic tradition of European culture, and stand committed to a policy of class war and social revolution. Yet it is obvious that any fresh shock to the stability of the European social and economic system is far more likely to hasten a collapse than to arrest it. The capitalist organization of industry and trade has played the same part in the unification of the modern world as the military organization of Rome did in antiquity, and Rome was saved not by revolutionaries like Spartacus or Catiline, but by men such as Julius Cæsar and Augustus, who converted Roman militarism from a destructive and selfish force into the servant of peace and world order. Europe to-day is waiting for its Augustus. It needs consolidation rather than revolution, but this consolidation cannot be the work of a military imperialism, as in the ancient world, it must be the fruit of social and economic co-operation between the different peoples and classes who make up the complex unity of European society.

There remains the Liberal tradition which seems at first sight more hopeful, since it stands for international peace and the old ideals of social freedom and progress. It is the spiritual parent of the League of Nations, the existence of which proves at least a general realization of the need for international co-operation and the possibility of a certain measure of common social activity. But the Liberal tradition no longer holds the dominant position that it had in the 19th century. It is still powerful as a practical force in the sphere of humanitarianism and social reform, and in politics it continues to exist, though it is everywhere fighting a losing battle with the parties of the Left and the Right. But in the intellectual world its reign is over. The

Liberal doctrines of progress and the perfectibility of society by purely rational means are no longer accepted as undisputed dogmas by the thinkers and writers of the present day. The scepticism and unbelief which in the heyday of Liberal enlightenment were directed against traditional religion have now been turned against the foundations of Liberalism itself.

And this development was inevitable, since, as we have seen, the Liberal faith owed its strength to the elements that it had derived from the religious tradition that it attempted to replace. Thus, in so far as it succeeded in secularizing European culture, it undermined the foundations on which its own existence depended. Instead of uniting Europe in a new spiritual unity, it had helped to destroy the spiritual tradition to which European culture owed its unity and its very existence.

II

And this brings us to a deeper problem than any of those we have already discussed, for it is upon the moral and spiritual unity of a culture that its external life ultimately depends. For Europe is not, as we have seen, a group of peoples held together by a common type of material culture, it is a spiritual society which owes its very existence to the religious tradition which for a thousand years moulded the beliefs, the ideals, and the institutions of the European peoples. Even the Reformation and the centuries of religious and international strife that followed it did not entirely destroy this common tradition. Europe remained Christendom, though it was a Christendom secularized and divided. The vision of its lost unity haunted the mind of Europe, and inspired the men of the 18th century with their enthusiasm for the abstract ideals of humanity and a new social order. They felt that Europe was being born again, and that the union of humanity was at hand.

But the new age saw the frustration of all these hopes. The vast progress of material civilization and of man's control over nature in the 19th century was not accompanied by corresponding advance in a spiritual unity. It seemed as though the new powers had outstripped all social control, and that man was becoming the slave of the machinery that he had created. While the ancient Greeks, or the men of the Middle Ages, had used their poor resources to create great artistic works as the material embodiment of their social and spiritual ideals, the men of the 19th century used their vast powers to build up the ugly, unhealthy, and disorderly cities of the industrial era, which seem devoid of form or of any common social purpose.

It is true that there was no decline in the activity of intellectual life, but here, also, there was a complete absence of cultural unity; science, religion, philosophy, and literature each went on its way regardless of the others. The mind of the age was divided against itself; it no longer possessed a common conception of reality capable of uniting the different activities of individual minds. This intellectual division and the consequent failure to achieve spiritual unity were the inevitable consequences of the spirit that had dominated European thought ever since the Reformation. They were, in fact, the price that modern culture had to pay for the conquest of nature and the immense progress of physical science.

For the downfall of the great mediæval synthesis destroyed the inner unity of European thought. It was a victory for physical science, which was emancipated from the dead hand of the Aristotelian cosmology, and left free to enter into its new heritage. But it was a defeat for philosophy, which now lost its former undisputed intellectual hegemony, and became a wanderer and an outcast, with no sure foothold in the world of reality. Like a discredited political leader, it was continually offering its services as a mediator between the opposing parties, only to be disavowed by both sides, and left to bear the responsibility for their blunders.

From the 17th century onwards the modern scientific movement has been based on the mechanistic view of nature which regards the world as a closed material order moved by purely mechanical and mathematical laws. All the aspects of reality which could not be reduced to mathematical terms and regarded as resulting from the blind operation of material forces were treated as mere subjective impressions of the human mind, and in so far as man himself was viewed as a by-product of this vast mechanical order, they were inevitably deprived of any ultimate reality.

A universe of this kind seems to leave no room for moral values or spiritual forces; indeed, it is hard to see what place the mind of the scientific observer himself has in the blind and endless flux of configurations of atoms which is the substance of reality. But, as we saw in the last chapter, the mind of the age refused to accept the consequences of a thorough-going

219

materialism, and combined its scientific determinism with a semi-philosophic, semi-theological Deism. The physical mechanism of the universe was not all. Outside it there also exists the Divine Engineer who had constructed the cosmic machinery, and who still supervises its working. In this way it was possible to conceive the universe in the spirit of strict scientific determinism while still preserving a belief in an ultimate teleology.[1]

Thus Deism provided a practical synthesis, but it was held together by an act of religious faith, rather than by any logical or metaphysical necessity. As Professor Whitehead has said: " While the Middle Ages were an age of faith based upon reason, the 18th century was an age of reason based upon faith." A great deal has been written during the last century on the conflict between religion and science, but the opposition of science and philosophy has really been much more fundamental. It is true that Comte, at least, attempted to create a philosophy which should be entirely positive and scientific, but in order to do this he had not only to abandon all metaphysics, but to purge science itself of all its abstract and theoretical elements and limit it to strictly practical ends. Thus all that he actually achieved was the synthesis of a partial aspect of science with an even more limited type of religion. On the other hand science has had little difficulty in coming to terms with religion, either in the form of abstract Deism, or of traditional Christianity. As a matter of fact a large number, perhaps

---

[1] This applies not only to Deism in the strict sense of the word, but also to the orthodox Deism of Christians like Newton and Priestley and Paley. In both cases the conception of the relation between God and the order of nature is essentially similar.

the majority, of the greatest scientists of modern times have been profoundly religious men, like Volta and Cauchy, Dalton and Faraday, Claude Bernard and Pasteur, Mendel and Wallace; while hardly one of them since the 18th century has been a philosopher. For strange as it may appear, a faith in the mechanistic hypothesis is far more easily reconcilable with a belief in theological dogmas than with any kind of metaphysical system.[1]

The Deist compromise broke down not because it was unscientific, but on account of its religious and philosophical weakness. Cut off from its roots in the living tradition of historic religion the Deist creed withered away from sheer lack of vitality. And its disappearance left the way clear for the consistent application of the mechanistic hypothesis to every aspect of existence. Man lost the privileged position which he had preserved in the world of Newton and the philosophers of the Enlightenment, and became part of the machine. The scientific determinism, which had at first been limited to the physical world, was now extended to biology and the social sciences. The 19th century economists, such as Ricardo and James Mill, conceived economic laws on the analogy of the mechanical laws of physical science, thus excluding all moral and spiritual factors and preparing the way for a "materialist interpretation of history." And in biology, Darwin himself was influenced both by the physicists and the economists in his central doctrine of

---

[1] Even the decline of the mechanistic view of nature has not entirely put an end to this state of things. For example, a biologist like Professor Julian Huxley, who is convinced of the possibility of a new religious interpretation of reality, refuses to admit the legitimacy of any metaphysical approach (see *Religion Without Revelation*, p. 138).

the evolution of species through the pressure of population on food supply and the consequent struggle for existence in which only the fittest survived.

But a world that is the product of chance and the blind working of material forces leaves no room for the golden hopes for the future of humanity which had been so characteristic of the 18th century creed. Even social reform and humanitarian ideals seemed difficult to reconcile with the mechanical view of social evolution, and the theory of the survival of the fittest was popularly interpreted in the crudely selfish form that used to be known to the French as " le struggleforlifeisme."

So long as science was the servant of the optimistic Deist creed, it was itself optimistic ; but as soon as science came into its kingdom its optimism began to disappear. Nor was this solely due to the influence of the Darwinian version of the evolutionary theory ; it lies in the very nature of the materialistic worldview. When once we abandon the theological doctrine of Creation, which is common both to orthodox Christianity and to the philosophic Deism which is derived from it, we are left with an eternal cosmic process, which does not admit of ultimate and absolute progress. The development of our planet is but a momentary result of material laws, which, working in infinite time and space, must repeat themselves endlessly, and so we are brought back to the cyclic theory of the Return of All Things, and once more we shall say with Lucretius : " Eadem sunt omnia semper."

And actually in the second half of the 19th century we begin once more to meet with new expressions of this most ancient doctrine. The passage in Nietzsche's *Joyful Wisdom* is well known, but it is worthy of repetition. " This life, as thou livest it now, as thou hast lived it, thou needst must live it again, and an infinite number of times; and there will be in it nothing new; but every grief and every joy, every thought and every sigh, all the infinitely great and the infinitely little in thy life must return for thee, and all this in the same sequence and the same order. And also this spider and the moonlight through the trees, and also this moment and myself. The eternal hour-glass of existence will ever be turned again, and thou with it, dust of dust."[1]

So, too, Auguste Blanqui, the Communist, wrote during his imprisonment in 1871 : " That which I write at this moment in a dungeon in the Fort of the Bull, I have written already, and I shall write it for eternity on the same table, with the same pen, in the same clothes and in the same circumstances. The universe repeats itself to infinity." [2]

It is hard to see how such a conclusion can be avoided on the mechanistic hypothesis, unless we accept Lord Kelvin's interpretation of the Law of the Degradation of Energy, according to which, not our planet, but the whole universe is slowly but inevitably travelling towards ultimate annihilation, since the energy that has once been dissipated or rendered inactive can never be reconstituted. The clock of nature is gradually running down, and so far as our knowledge goes, there is no natural process by which it can ever be wound up again. Thus the cosmic process is apparently not circular, as the Greeks believed, but moves in a single

---

[1] *The Joyful Wisdom*, no. 341. In this passage the idea is stated hypothetically, but it is more definitely affirmed in *Werke* XII, 122.
[2] A Blanqui, *L'Eternité par les astres*, 1872. cf. A. Rey, *le retour éternel et la philosophie de la physique*, 1927.

irreversible direction. It has a beginning, and must ultimately have an end, though in the intervening period there is room for an uncounted number of worlds and cycles. Change is not mere illusion, it is the ultimate reality of the physical universe.

Nevertheless, the idea of an absolute beginning or end is so repugnant to anyone who does not accept a theistic or non-mechanical world view, that it has never been fully assimilated by the modern scientific mind. From Herbert Spencer and Haeckel to Arrhenius and Becquerel and Abel Rey there has been a whole series of attempts to provide new scientific justification for the mechanistic theory of an eternal recurrence; and there is no reason to think that the cyclical theory has been finally abandoned.

Thus the only ultimate progress conceivable in a mechanistic universe is a progress to eternal death. Nor is this the only difficulty which arises from the abandonment of the old theological optimism. It reacted disastrously upon men's conception of the objective value of science. As we have seen, the rise of modern physics was closely connected with a transcendental view of the nature of mathematics derived from the Pythagorean and Platonic tradition. According to this view, God created the world in accordance with numerical harmonies, and consequently it is only by the science of number that it can be understood. " Just as the eye was made to see colours," says Kepler, " and the ear to hear sounds, so the human mind was made to understand Quantity." (*Opera I*, 31.) And Galileo describes mathematics as the script in which God has written on the open book of the Universe. But this philosophy of mathematics which underlies the old science, requires a deity to guarantee its truth. If the laws of mathematics are simply the creation of the human mind, they are no infallible guide to the ultimate nature of things. They are a conventional technique which is no more based on the eternal laws of the universe than is the number of degrees in a circle or the number of yards in a mile. Physical science, in fact, is nothing more or less than measurement. It does not reveal the intrinsic nature of things, but deals simply with their quantitative relations and variations. Instead of giving an exhaustive causal explanation of reality, it offers a translation of reality into mathematical symbols or imagery. Thus scientific laws have the same relation to nature that the printed score of one of Beethoven's sonatas has to the music, or as Professor Eddington has said, they have as much resemblance to the real qualities of nature that a telephone number has to the individual subscriber whom it represents.[1]

It is true that this recognition of the limitations of science is as yet almost entirely confined to the mathematicians and the physicists. It has not reached the biologists and the psychologists, who still tend to regard natural science as capable of giving a complete and exhaustive explanation of reality. It is obvious that the biologist is even less able to explain the nature of life, than is the physicist to explain that of the atom. But he is more apt to believe that he can do so, because his science is less completely mathe-

---

[1] This criticism of the nature and conditions of scientific knowledge has been mainly the work of the scientists themselves, such as Duhem and Henri Poincaré in France, and more recently Professor Eddington and Professor Whitehead in this country. The subject is most completely dealt with from the philosophic point of view by E. Meyerson *De l'explication dans les Sciences*, 2 vols. 1921.

maticized. It deals not with algebraical symbols but with looser and vaguer concepts, such as life, organism and species, which have acquired a certain non-scientific richness of content from the experience of daily life. And the psychologist and the sociologist are worse offenders, since they are working on subjects which are far less amenable to exact scientific treatment, and are proportionately more dependent on empirical ideas. Nevertheless this popular idealization of natural science as the exclusive source of our knowledge of reality is ultimately dependent on its acceptance by the physicists who were originally responsible for it. And consequently the adoption of a new and more exact conception of the nature and limits of the scientific method by the physicists themselves portends a profound revolution in thought. It undermines the old scientific determinism which was based on the assumption that science can give an exhaustive knowledge of the causes of things, and it destroys even more completely the naïve concreteness of the materialistic attitude to nature. In the past, science conceived matter as a genuine *substance* the existence of which was a fact of sensible experience.[1] To-day the solid world of the materialist has vanished in a tenuous web of mathematical formulæ. The common-sense dogmatism of the old-fashioned materialist would find the abstract conceptions of modern physics no less difficult to assimi-

---

[1] " The Victorian physicist felt that he knew just what he was talking about when he used such terms as *matter* and *atoms*. Atoms were tiny billiard balls, a crisp statement that was supposed to tell you all about their nature in a way that could never be achieved for transcendental things like consciousness, beauty or humour. But now we realise that science has nothing to say as to the intrinsic nature of the atom. The physical atom is like everything else in physics, a schedule of pointer readings." A. S. Eddington. *The Nature of the Physical World.* p. 259.

late than the subtleties of the old metaphysicians. From the point of view of science, this is pure gain, since it means that scientific thought has purified itself from the bastard quasi-metaphysical conceptions which were masquerading as scientific truths. But from the sociological point of view this advance is not without its penalties. The achievement of the last two centuries would hardly have been possible had there not existed a view of the universe and of the nature of reality which was easily comprehensible to the average man and equally accepted by the men of science. At present no such common world view is possible, and modern science is poised insecurely on the verge of a metaphysical abyss which is continually threatening to engulf it. For the more rigidly the province of science is defined and its claims are limited, the more pressing becomes the need for a metaphysical or rather meta-scientific explanation of reality.

But if science cannot take the place of philosophy, still less can it act as a substitute for religion. It is in vain that we look to science for a power which will unite and guide the divided forces of European society. Science provides, not a moral dynamic, but an intellectual technique. It is entirely indifferent to moral considerations, and lends itself with sublime impartiality to any power which knows how to use it—like the Slave of the Ring in the *Arabian Nights*, who is equally ready " to build a town or to ruin a city, or to slay a King or to dig a river or anything else of the kind." It is true that during the last century science has well served the cause of humanity in countless ways, but this is precisely because it has been the servant of the humanitarian spirit which, as we have seen, was not the product of science but of a distinctly religious tradition.

It may, of course, be argued that the disappearance of this tradition in no way affects the practical value of science, and that the renunciation of all religious and metaphysical dogmas will leave us free to use the resources of science for positive social ends. As the 18th century abandoned dogmatic religion and still continued to advance in material culture, why should not the 20th century get on well enough without the liberal idealism which is merely an unsubstantial shadow projected from the religion of the past?

This is indeed what the world seems to be doing to-day. We have entered on a new phase of culture—we may call it the Age of the Cinema—in which the most amazing perfection of scientific technique is being devoted to purely ephemeral objects, without any consideration of their ultimate justification. It seems as though a new society was arising which will acknowledge no hierarchy of values, no intellectual authority, and no social or religious tradition, but which will live for the moment in a chaos of pure sensation.

Such a society is by no means inconceivable. It had its counterpart in the great cities of the Roman Empire, which lived for the games of the amphitheatre and the circus. But it is obvious that a civilization of this kind holds no promise for the future save that of social disintegration. Moreover, the fact that religion no longer finds a place in social life does not necessarily involve the disappearance of the religious instinct. If the latter is denied its normal expression, and driven back upon itself, it may easily become an anti-social force of explosive violence.

We have already seen how the secularization of European culture was accompanied by a kind of social apocalypticism which gave rise to a new type of social unrest. Political disturbances are as old as human nature. In every age misgovernment and oppression has been met by violence and disorder, but it is a new thing, and perhaps a phenomenon peculiar to our modern Western civilization, that men should work and think and agitate for the complete remodelling of society according to some ideal of social perfection. It belongs to the order of religion, rather than to that of politics, as politics were formerly understood. It finds its only parallel in the past in movements of the most extreme religious type, like that of the Anabaptists in 16th century Germany and the Levellers and Fifth Monarchy Men of Puritan England. And when we study the lives of the founders of modern Socialism, the great Anarchists, and even some of the apostles of the Nationalist Liberalism, like Mazzini, we feel at once that we are in the presence of religious leaders, whether prophets or heresiarchs, saints or fanatics. Behind the hard rational surface of Karl Marx's materialist and socialist interpretation of history, there burns the flame of an apocalyptic vision. For what was that social revolution in which he put his hope but a 19th century version of the Day of the Lord, in which the rich and the powerful of the earth should be consumed and the princes of the Gentiles brought low, and the poor and disinherited should reign in a regenerated universe?

So, too, Marx, in spite of his professed atheism, looked for the realization of this hope, not like St. Simon and his fellow " idealist " socialists, to the conversion

229

of the individual and to human efforts towards the attainment of a new social ideal, but to " the arm of the Lord," the necessary, ineluctable working out of the Eternal Law, which human will and human effort are alike powerless to change or stay.

But the religious impulse behind these social movements is not a constructive one. It is as absolute in its demands as that of the old religions, and it admits of no compromise with reality. As soon as the victory is gained and the phase of destruction and revolution is ended, the inspiration fades away before the tasks of practical realization. We look in vain in the history of united Italy for the religious enthusiasm that sustained Mazzini and his fellows, and it took very few years to transform the Rousseauan idealism of revolutionary France, the Religion of Humanity, into Napoleonic and even Machiavellian realism.

The revolutionary attitude—and it is perhaps the characteristic religious attitude of Modern Europe—is in fact nothing but a symptom of the divorce between religion and social life. The 19th century revolutionaries—the anarchists, the socialists, and to some extent the liberals—were driven to their destructive activities by the sense that actual European society was a mere embodiment of material force and fraud —" magnum latrocinium," as St. Augustine says— that it was based on no principle of justice, and organized for no spiritual or ideal end; and the more the simpler and more obvious remedies—Republicanism, Universal Suffrage, National Self-Determination— proved disappointing to the reformers, the deeper became their dissatisfaction with the whole structure of existing society. And so, finally, when the process of disillusionment is complete, this religious impulse that lies behind the revolutionary attitude may turn itself against social life altogether, or at least against the whole system of civilization that has been built up in the last two centuries. This attitude of mind seems endemic in Russia, partly perhaps as an inheritance from the Byzantine religious tradition.[1] We see it appearing in different forms in Tolstoi, in Dostoievski, and in the Nihilists, and it is present as a psychic undercurrent in most of the Russian revolutionary movements. It is the spirit, which seeks not political reform, not the improvement of social conditions, but escape, liberation—Nirvana. In the words of a modern poet (Francis Adams), it is " To wreck the great guilty temple, and give us Rest."

And in the years since the war, when the failure of the vast machinery of modern civilization has seemed so imminent, this view of life has become more common even in the West. It has inspired the work of the Austrian poet, Albert Ehrenstein,[2] and many others.

It may seem to some that these instances are negligible, mere morbid extravagances, but it is impossible to exaggerate the dangers that must inevitably arise when once social life has become separated from the religious impulse.

We have only to look at the history of the ancient world and we shall see how tremendous are these consequences. The Roman Empire, and the Hellenistic

---

[1] cf. M. Zdziechowski: *Le Dualisme dans la pensée religieuse russe;* and N. Berdiaeff: *L'Idée religieuse russe;* both in *les Cahiers de la Nouvelle Journée,* viii, 1927.

[2] For instance, the following verse:—
Ich beschwöre euch, zerstampfet die Stadt.
Ich beschwöre euch, zertrümmert die Städte.
Ich beschwöre euch, zerstört die Maschine.
Ich beschwöre euch, zerstöret den Staat.

civilization of which it was the vehicle, became separated in this way from any living religious basis, which all the efforts of Augustus and his helpers were powerless to restore, and thereby, in spite of its high material and intellectual culture, the dominant civilization became hateful in the eyes of the subject Oriental world. Rome was to them not the ideal world-city of Virgil's dream, but the incarnation of all that was anti-spiritual, Babylon the great, the mother of Abominations, who bewitched and enslaved all the peoples of the earth, and on whom at last the slaughter of the saints and the oppression of the poor would be terribly avenged. And so all that was strongest and most living in the moral life of the time separated itself from the life of society and from the service of the State, as from something unworthy and even morally evil. Thus we see in Egypt in the 4th century, over against the great Hellenic city of Alexandria, filled with art and learning and all that made life delightful, a new power growing up, the power of the men of the desert, the naked, fasting monks and ascetics, in whom, nevertheless, the new world recognised its masters. When, in the 5th century, the greatest of the late Latin writers summed up the history of the great Roman tradition, it is in a spirit of profound hostility and disillusionment : " Acceperunt mercedem suam," says he in an unforgettable sentence, " vani vanam."

This spiritual alienation of its own greatest minds is the price that every civilization has to pay when it loses its religious foundations, and is contented with a a purely material success. We are only just beginning to understand how intimately and profoundly the vitality of a society is bound up with its religion. It is the religious impulse which supplies the cohesive force which unifies a society and a culture. The great civilizations of the world do not produce the great religions as a kind of cultural by-product; in a very real sense the great religions are the foundations on which the great civilizations rest. A society which has lost its religion becomes sooner or later a society which has lost its culture.

X

CONCLUSION

WE have followed the development of human culture through the ages, and have seen how at every step
the religion of a society expresses its dominant attitude
to life and its ultimate conception of reality. Religion
is the great dynamic force in social life, and the vital
changes in civilization are always linked with changes
in religious beliefs and ideals. The secularization of
a society involves the devitalization of that society, for,
as Péguy said, the passing of a religion is not a sign
of progress, but a token of social decay.[1] Our own
civilization to an even greater extent than those of the
past has been the creation of a religious tradition, for
it is to Christianity that Europe owes its cultural unity.
And for fifteen hundred years the spiritual dynamic
of Western culture has been drawn from the same
source, whether directly in the traditional Christian
form, or indirectly through the survival of Christian
ideals in Liberalism and the Religion of Progress.

But the religious tradition is not identical with that
of our culture in the sense in which Hinduism embraces

[1] " Quand le groupe des metaphysiques et des religions, des philosophies
masquées decroît derrière des coteaux que l'humanité ne reverra sans doute
jamais, en vérité ne nous rejouissons pas: car symétriquement et solidairement
c'est nous aussi qui décroissons." Charles Péguy *cahier dit de l'ensevelissement
d'Hypatie, Cahiers de la Quinzaine*, viii, 11.

234

the whole civilization of India, or Mohammedanism that of the Islamic peoples. Our civilization has a peculiar duality which is not found among the simpler and more homogeneous cultures of the East, or those of the ancient world. There is a second element—the scientific tradition—which is even older than Christianity, since it has its origins in the Hellenic culture of classical times, and which has, to some extent, followed an independent line of development. It does not possess that dynamic social power which is the peculiar characteristic of religion, but nevertheless it has conditioned the whole development of our culture and has given Europe a power of material organization and control over nature that no other civilization has possessed. Nor is this tradition limited to physical science; its influence is seen also in the development of Western philosophy, in mediæval scholasticism, in Roman law and in modern political and social organization. Everywhere it seeks to bring order and intelligibility alike into the material world and into the world of thought.

It is not surprising that there should be a tendency in modern times to regard this second element as the true European tradition, and to treat Christianity as an alien religious tradition which had temporarily deflected the normal development of our culture. As a matter of fact, neither the religious nor the scientific tradition of the West are the result of a spontaneous *native* development in the same way that Confucianism was the product of China, or the philosophy of the Vedanta was the creation of India. Western Europe was first incorporated into a cultural unity by the coming of Christianity, and it was only in consequence

235

of that development that the West became capable of inheriting also the rational tradition of the Hellenic culture. The scientific tradition has never been the dynamic force in our civilization, and we have seen that the naïve 19th century belief in modern physical science as a substitute for religion, as expressed, for example, by Renan in *L'Avenir de la Science*, is founded on a misapprehension of the nature of science itself.

Nevertheless, since the two traditions are distinct in origin, there still remains the possibility that they are not mutually consistent, and that a more complete synthesis might be achieved if a more rational and naturalistic religious doctrine was substituted for the supernaturalism of Christian dogma. In this sense, there is nothing illogical in the idea of a " religion of science," provided that it be clearly recognised that it belongs to the realm of religion and not to that of science. In the past, as we have seen, it is the rule rather than the exception for religion to concern itself with the knowledge of nature. The very origins of science are to be found among the medicine men and priesthoods of primitive people, and at a higher stage of civilization cosmological speculation occupies a considerable place in the development of the great religions.

The religion of China, for example, is founded on a theory of the order of nature and of the positive and negative principles whose alternation produces the cosmic process, and this theory also forms the foundation of Chinese science. So, too, in Greece, the religion of Plato was essentially a religion of science, since he regarded scientific knowledge, and above all mathematics, as a religious discipline and a pathway to spiritual perfection. Indeed, he went further in this direction than any other thinker by his bold attempt to rationalize the popular religion, and to substitute astronomy for mythology as the basis of a new state cultus.

But a philosophic religion of the Platonic type is not at all the kind of thing which the modern seekers after a religion of science have in view. It is just the Platonic attitude to religion and life which is most antipathetic to them, and their criticism of the existing forms of religion is largely directed against the metaphysical element in them. They demand that religion shall come back to earth—to an immediate contact with nature and man, and give up its vain pursuit of the mirage of the Absolute. Indeed, there are not wanting those who believe that the whole movement of the world religions has been a mistake— a blind alley on the path of human development—and that we must return to the older attitude to nature and life which the higher civilization abandoned more than two thousand years ago. From this point of view the religion of the future will be a kind of neo-paganism which will consist in the worship of the vital forces of nature in place of spiritual abstractions or of a transcendent divinity. The religious attitude to nature will be the same as in the paganism of the past, but scientific law will take the place of the system of ritual magic on which the old civilizations relied in order to bring human life into communion with the cosmic order. Some experiments in this direction have actually been made—for example, at Indore, a few years ago, the Diwali festival was utilized as a means of sanitary propaganda, and the spirit of Dirt, personified as the demon Narakasur, the enemy of Rama, was solemnly burnt.[1] But though such attempts may succeed in cases where the traditional nature worship still exists, it is very unlikely that they can ever meet with acceptance where this element is lacking. The religion of Comte, with its worship of Humanity, the Great Being, and of the Earth, the Great Fetish, was an utter failure, in spite of the powerful philosophic synthesis on which it was based. When man has once tasted of the Tree of Knowledge, he cannot go back to the paradise of the primitive. It was possible for the latter to divinize the forces of nature and to adopt a truly religious attitude towards them, because they still belonged to the realm of mystery, and were regarded as manifestations of a power that was not merely natural. But as soon as man had gained a certain measure of control over his environment and had learnt to regard nature as amenable to human reason and will, the old naïve attitude of awe and worship was gone for ever. Henceforward man was the master in his own house, and he could no longer admit the supremacy of any non-rational power. And it is well that he cannot, since to do so would be to wipe out half the experience of the race.

A religious movement which attempted to turn its back on the spiritual achievement of the last three thousand years would be far more retrograde than any antiscientific reaction to the historic religions of the past.

Yet it must be admitted that the modern criticism of the great world religions is not altogether devoid of foundation. Their intellectual absolutism and their concentration on metaphysical conceptions have tended

---

[1] Cf. V. Branford, *Hinduism in Transition* in *Living Religions*, 1924.

to turn men's minds away from the material world, and from practical social activity. But this pre-occupation with the Eternal and the Absolute and the spirit of "otherworldiness" which it generates is antipathetic to the modern mind, since it seems ultimately to destroy the value and signification of relative knowledge—that is to say of natural science—and of human life itself. The present age seems to demand a religion which will be an incentive to action and a justification of the material and social progress which has been the peculiar achievement of the last two centuries.

An attempt to supply this need is to be found in the new theories of evolutionary vitalism which are so popular in philosophic circles at the present time. The movement originated with Bergson's philosophy of creative evolution, but it has had a much wider development in this country than on the Continent. It is represented, on the one hand, by the doctrine of " Emergent Evolution " put forward by Professor Alexander and Professor Lloyd Morgan, and on the other by the pantheistic vitalism of scientists like Professors Julian Huxley and J. H. Haldane. According to the theory of the former, the spiritual values on which the world religions were based are not illusory. They have a real place in the universe, but they are not absolute and transcendental realities, as the old religions believed. They are, no less than material things, the result of an evolutionary process. Thus God is not the creator of the world, he is himself created with the world, or rather he " emerges " as part of the cosmic process. In Professor Alexander's words, " God as an actual existent is always becoming deity, but never attains it,

He is the ideal God in embryo. The ideal when fulfilled ceases to be God."[1]

Professor Huxley's position, on the other hand, is not a philosophical one. He professes a complete Spencerian agnosticism with regard to metaphysical problems, and seeks to find the material for a religious interpretation of reality in natural science and in human nature itself. His aim is a strictly religious one, and he is concerned to a far greater extent than any of the other writers that we have mentioned with the discovery of a religious solution which will satisfy the moral and social needs of modern civilization.

Nevertheless, in spite of this difference of standpoint, his religious ideal is not unlike that of Professor Alexander. Science, he believes, teaches us that the world is advancing in a spiritual direction. The process of evolution has no spiritual creative power behind it, but in man matter has flowered in spirit, and spiritual values have " emerged " from the blind movement of material forces. Consequently the religious impulse must find its satisfaction in a conscious co-operation with this cosmic trend. God is the human ideal, but inasmuch as man is the vanguard of nature's advance, his ideal is an earnest of future achievement. " It is Incarnate Spirit," he says, " embodied in Life the Mediator."[2] Or again in one of his earlier sonnets:

" The Universe can live and work and plan
    At last made God within the mind of Man."[3]

[1] S. Alexander: *Space, Time and Deity*, vol. II, p. 365. cf. p. 361. " The infinite God is purely ideal or conceptual. . . . As actual, God does not possess the quality of deity but is the universe as tending to that quality."
[2] *Religion Without Revelation* (1927), p. 329.
[3] *God and Man* in *Essays of a Biologist* (1923), p. 234.

It is clear that Professor Huxley's religious ideal is simply that of the Religion of Progress in a new form. But though his theory of a divine ideal, immanent in the life process itself, avoids the external dogmatism of the Deist creed, it brings fresh difficulties in its train. The old teleological interpretation of nature has been abandoned only to be replaced by an attempt to read spiritual values into biology and the evolutionary process. Such an interpretation will always tend to reflect the metaphysical and theological preconceptions of its author. The *élan vital* of Bergson, for example, is not a pure generalization of biological facts, it is rather the explanation of those facts by a quasi-theological hypothesis, half way between the Stoic theory of a World Soul and the Christian doctrine of the Holy Ghost. In the case of Professor Huxley's interpretation, the derivation of his religious symbolism from the Christian doctrine of the Trinity is quite conscious and deliberate. But although he has attempted to free it from all theistic or metaphysical connotations, it is obviously something more than a mere symbolic formula. It involves a real contact with the religious attitude and the spiritual tradition of Christianity.

For the conception of the progressive spiritualization of nature—the embodiment of a divine principle in the order of time—is not the only or the most obvious deduction to be drawn from the contemplation of the evolutionary process. In the presence of the same facts, a Hindu would see, not the gradual emergence of the human ethical ideal, but the manifestation of a universal cosmic energy which is no less divine in its destructive and malevolent aspects than in its beneficent

241

ones—in which all values are alike because they are all the expressions of a single creative fecundity. It is Shiva, the Terrible One, dancing his cosmic dance amidst the birth and death of the worlds. And this interpretation of life which finds God in the whole cosmic process is at least as logical as that of the European idealist who sees God only in the human mind— that is in the mental processes of a single species of mammalia. Moreover, it seems equally capable of evoking intense religious emotion, as we see in countless Shivaite and Saktist prayers and hymns.[1]

To us these conceptions are unacceptable. They seem definitely lower and less true than the idea of the world process as a gradual ascent in a spiritual direction. But this is because we view the evolutionary process through Christian eyes, even when, like Professor Huxley, we profess the most complete religious agnosticism.

For the moral idealism which is still so characteristic of the Western mind is the fruit of an age-long tradition of religious faith and spiritual discipline. Humanitarianism is the peculiar possession of a people who have worshipped for centuries the Divine Humanity —apart from all that even our humanism would have been other than it is. It is from this Christian moral tradition that both the older Deist movement and the new movement of evolutionary vitalism have derived whatever positive religious value they possess. Never-

---

[1] Cf. for example the following lines of Tirunavukkarasu Swami (in *Hymn of the Tamil Saivite Saints*, tr. Kingsbury and Philips, p. 53):

"Head of mine bow to Him,
True Head, skull garlanded
. . . .
Bow low to Him, my head."

theless this element cannot continue to exist indefinitely, if it is divorced from the historic religious beliefs on which it is really founded.

The Deist attempt to found a natural religion broke down because it was the result of a superficial synthesis, which only succeeded in uniting the etiolated ghost of historic Christianity with the phantasm of a pseudo-scientific rationalism. It claimed to be the Religion of Nature, when it was as abstract and artificial as any metaphysical system. It professed to base itself on purely rational grounds, when it really drew its spiritual vitality from the religious tradition that it rejected. It was neither truly religious nor completely rational, and consequently it was rejected alike by the most living religion and by the most serious scientific thought of the new age.

But if the Religion of Progress failed to establish itself, after it had captured public opinion, and had the whole tendency of the new age in its favour, it is hardly likely that it will be more successful in this age of disillusionment in its new form of evolutionary vitalism. For the latter suffers from the same fundamental weaknesses and inconsistencies, while it lacks the power of popular appeal which was the main strength of the older movement.

The day of the Liberal Deist compromise is over, and we have come to the parting of the ways. Either Europe must abandon the Christian tradition and with it the faith in progress and humanity, or it must return consciously to the religious foundation on which these ideas were based. The modern world has not lost its need for religion—indeed the value and the necessity of a religious interpretation of life are felt

243

more strongly than they were fifty years ago, and science no longer attempts, as it did then, to deny their legitimacy. But the religious impulse must express itself openly through religious channels, instead of seeking a furtive, illegitimate expression in scientific and political theories to the detriment alike of religion and science. It must be recognized that our faith in progress and in the unique value of human experience rests on religious foundations, and that they cannot be severed from historical religion and used as a substitute for it, as men have attempted to do during the last two centuries.

It is true that there still exists a widespread prejudice against any religion which claims to rest on divine or supernatural revelation. The old 18th century ideal of a purely rational religion—a Religion without Revelation—has not lost its attractiveness to the modern mind.

But a religion without Revelation is a religion without History, and it is just the historical element in Christianity which gives it its peculiar character, and differentiates it from the unprogressive metaphysical religions of the East. A purely rational religion must inevitably become a metaphysical religion, for the religious impulse can find no nourishment for itself in the arid and narrow region of the discursive reason, and it is only in the metaphysical sphere—in the intuition of absolute and eternal truth—that religion and reason can meet.

On the other hand the religious instinct finds its fullest and most concrete satisfaction in the historical field—through faith in an historical person, an historical community, and an historical tradition.

No religion can entirely dispense with this element. Even in so abstract and metaphysical a faith as that of Buddhism, an intense religious emphasis is attached to the historical personality of the Buddha himself. Nevertheless in all the oriental religions, as well as in the abstract philosophical religious movements of the West, this element is subordinated to the metaphysical aspect of religion. It is only in Christianity that the historic element acquires such importance that it can be wholly identified with the transcendent and eternal objects of religious faith. The Christian, and he alone, can find a solution to the paradox of the inherence of eternity in time, and of the absolute in the finite which does not empty human life and the material world of their religious significance and value.

Hence it is in historic Christianity, far more than in any purely rational creed, that the Religion of Progress finds its satisfaction. For here we have not an abstract intellectualized progress, but the emergence of new spiritual values in a concrete historical sense. A new *kind* of life has inserted itself into the cosmic process at a particular point in time under definite historical circumstances and has become the principle of a new order of spiritual progress.

The creative process which has reached its end in man starts off again *from* man in a second ascent, the possibilities of which are as yet unrealized, and which are to be grasped not by Reason, which lives on the systematization of the past, but by Faith, which is the promise of the future.

Nor is it only in regard to these ultimate problems that the Religion of Progress finds its fulfilment in Christianity. The practical humanitarian aims of that movement, which are responsible for the social reforms of the last two centuries, also need the support of a positive religious tradition. The ideal of a social order based on justice and goodwill between men and nations has not lost its attraction for the European mind, but with the disappearance of the old Liberal optimism it is in danger of being abandoned as a visionary illusion, unless it is reinforced by a renewal of spiritual conviction. For it is a religious ideal and cannot exist without some religious foundation.

The return to the historic Christian tradition would restore to our civilization the moral force that it requires in order to dominate external circumstances and to avoid the dangers that are inherent in the present situation. We have seen that science is unable to realize all its vast potentialities for the organization and transformation of human existence, unless it is directed by a moral purpose which it does not itself possess. And it can find this dynamic in a true historic religion such as Christianity as well, or even better than, in an artificial " religion of science," which is a mere *deus ex machina* for solving a temporary intellectual problem and possesses no spiritual vitality of its own.

It is true that the great historic religions of the East do seem to justify in some measure the rationalist's view of the incompatibility of religion with science, since they deny the reality or the importance of the material world. They tend to withdraw themselves to the heights of pure intelligence and leave the sensible world in confusion and anarchy. But Christianity is not committed to this oriental and metaphysical tradition, however far certain periods and schools of

246

thought may have gone in that direction. It has always resisted the Gnostic or Manichæan tendency to regard the material world as intrinsically evil. It seeks not the destruction or the negation of nature, but its spiritualization and its incorporation in a higher order of reality. Consequently the organization of the material world by science and law which has been the characteristic task of modern European culture is in no sense alien to the genius of Christianity. For the progressive intellectualization of the material world which is the work of European science is analogous and complementary to the progressive spiritualization of human nature which is the function of the Christian religion. The future of humanity depends on the harmony and co-ordination of these two processes.

Hitherto, it must be admitted, this harmony has never been fully achieved by any historic civilization. During the Middle Ages Europe was still largely dominated by the semi-oriental traditions of the Byzantine culture, and it was only in the age of St. Francis and St. Thomas Aquinas that the West began to attain spiritual and intellectual independence. And since the Renaissance, our civilization has increasingly lost touch with the religious tradition, and has become absorbed in its task of material organization to the detriment of its moral and spiritual unity. Nevertheless, it is to the co-existence of these two elements that Europe owes the distinctive character of its culture. From Christianity it has derived its moral unity and its social ideals, while science has given it its power of material organization and its control over nature. Without religion, science becomes a neutral

247

force which lends itself to the service of militarism and economic exploitation as readily as to the service of humanity. Without science, on the other hand, society becomes fixed in an immobile, unprogressive order, like that of the Byzantine culture and the Oriental civilizations in general. It is only through the co-operation of both these forces that Europe can realize its latent potentialities and enter on a new phase of civilization which is equally removed from the sterile inaction of the ancient East and the aimless material activity of the modern West.

And the return to the Christian tradition would provide Europe with the necessary spiritual foundation for the social unification that it so urgently needs. We have seen that Europe has never possessed the natural unity of the other great cultures. It has owed its unity, and its very existence as a distinct civilization, to its membership of a common spiritual society. And perhaps that is the reason why it has never been able to be satisfied with a purely political unification. No doubt a giant supernational state would bring Europe relief from many of her practical problems, but it would also involve the sacrifice of many of the ideals that she has most prized. But this is not the only solution. It is possible that the ideal form of international unity for Europe is not a political one at all, but a spiritual one. After all, the state is not the only form of social unity. " Let us not forget," wrote Nietzsche, " in the end what a Church is, and especially in contrast to every " state " : a Church is above all an authoritative organization which secures to the most *spiritual* men the highest rank, and *believes* in the power of spirituality so far as to forbid all grosser appliances of authority.

248

Through this alone the Church is under all circumstances a *nobler* institution than the State."[1]

At the present moment such a solution appears inconceivable. We have come to take it for granted that the unifying force in society is material interest, and that spiritual conviction is a source of strife and division. Modern civilization has pushed religion and the spiritual elements in culture out of the main stream of its development, so that they have lost touch with social life and have become sectarianized and impoverished. But at the same time this has led to the impoverishment of our whole culture. It has borne fruit in that " plebeianism of the European spirit " which Nietzche regarded as the necessary consequence of the disappearance of the spiritual power.

This, however, is but a temporary phenomenon; it can never be the normal condition of humanity. For, as we have seen, the vital and creative power behind every culture is a spiritual one. In proportion as the spiritual element recovers its natural position at the centre of our culture, it will necessarily become the mainspring of our whole social activity. This does not, however, mean that the material and spiritual aspects of life must become fused in a single political order which would have all the power and rigidity of a theocratic state. Since a culture is essentially a spiritual community; it transcends the economic and political orders. It finds its appropriate organ not in a state, but in a Church, that is to say a society which is the embodiment of a purely spiritual tradition and which rests, not on material power, but on the free adhesion of the individual mind. It has been the

[1] *The Joyful Wisdom.* Eng. trans., p. 314.

peculiar achievement of Western Christianity in the past to realize such an ideal in an organized spiritual society, which could co-exist with the national political units without either absorbing or being absorbed by them. The return to this tradition would once more make it possible to reconcile the existence of national independence and political freedom, which are an essential part of European life, with the wider unity of our civilization, and with that higher process of spiritual integration which is the true goal of human progress.

THE END

BIBLIOGRAPHY

BRANFORD, V., and GEDDES, P. "The Coming Polity," 1917.

BRUNET, G. "Le Mysticisme Social de Saint-Simon," 1925.

BURTT, E. A. "The Metaphysical Foundations of Modern Physical Science," 1925.

BURY, J. B. "The Idea of Progress," 1920.

COMTE, I. A. M. F. X. "Cours de Philosophie Positive," 6 vols., 1830–42.

—— "Système de Politique Positive," 4 vols., 1851–4.

CONDORCET, M. J. N. C. de. "Esquisse d'un tableau historique des progrès de l'esprit humain," 1795.

DELVAILLE, J. "Essai sur l'histoire de l'idée de progrès jusqu'à la fin du 18ième siècle," 1910.

DUHEM, P. "Le système du monde de Platon à Copernie," 5 vols., 1913–17.

EDDINGTON, A. S. "The Nature of the Physical World," 1928.

FICHTE, J. G. "The Characteristics of the Present Age" (1806), trans. W. Smith, 1847.

FLINT, R. "Philosophy of History in Europe," Vol. I, 1874.

—— "History of the Philosophy of History," Vol. I, 1893.

FRAZER, J. G. "Lectures on the Early History of Kingship," 1905.

—— "The Golden Bough," 12 vols.

—— "Psyche's Task : A discourse on the influence of superstition on the growth of institutions," 1909.

251

HEGEL, G. W. F. " Lectures on the Philosophy of History," trans. J. Sibree, 1857.

HOBHOUSE, L. T. " Development and Purpose," 1913.

—— " Social Evolution and Political Theory," 1911.

HUBY, J. (ed.) " Christus : Manuel d'histoire des religions," 1916.

HUXLEY, J. " Essays of a Biologist," 1923 (including an essay on Progress).

—— " Religion without Revelation," 1927.

HUXLEY, T. H. " Evolution and Ethics " (Vol. IX of Collected Essays, 1893–4).

INGE, W. R. " The Idea of Progress " (Romanes Lecture), 1920.

KROEBER, A. L. " Anthropology," 1923.

LANG, A. " The Making of Religion," 1878.

—— " Myth, Ritual, and Religion," 2nd ed., 2 vols., 1899.

LE PLAY, P. G. F. " Les Ouvriers Européens," 6 vols., 1877–9.

LEROUX, P. " De l'humanité," 2 vols., 1840.

LESSING, G. E. " The Education of the Human Race " (1777–80), trans. F. W. Robertson.

LOWIE, R. H. " Primitive Society," 1921.

—— " Primitive Religion, " 1925.

MARRETT, R. R. " The Threshold of Religion," 2nd ed., 1914.

MARVIN, F. S. (ed.) " Progress and History," 1921.

—— —— " The Century of Hope," 1919.

—— —— " Science and Civilization," 1923.

MERZ, J. T. " History of European Thought in the Nineteenth Century," 4 vols., 1896–1914.

MEYERSON, E. " De l'explication dans les sciences," 2 vols., 1921.

MORLEY, J. " Rousseau," 2 vols., 1873.

—— Essays on Condorcet and Turgot in "Miscellanies," Vol. II, 1886.

OTTO, R. "Das Heilige; Über das Irrationale in der Idee des Göttlichen und sein Verhältnis zum Rationale," 1917 (15th ed. 1926), (trans. by J. W. Harvey, "The Idea of the Holy," 1923).

PÉGUY, C. "De la situation faite à l'histoire et à la sociologie et de la situation faite au parti intellectuel dans le monde moderne," 1907.

PINARD DE LA BOULLAYE, H. "L'Étude comparée des religions," 2 vols., 1922–5.

RADIN, P. "Primitive Man as Philosopher," 1927.

RIVERS, W. H. R. "The History of Melanesian Society," 2 vols., 1914.

—— "Psychology and Politics," 1923.

—— "History and Ethnology," 1922.

SCHLEGEL, C. W. F. VON. "The Philosophy of History" (1828), trans. J. B. Robertson, 2nd ed., 1846.

SÖDERBLOM, N. "Das Werden des Gottesglauben" (German trans.), 1916.

SPENCER, H. "The Principles of Sociology," 3 vols., 1876–96.

—— "Social Statics," 1851.

—— "The Study of Sociology," 9th ed., 1880.

SPENGLER, O. "Der Untergang des Abendlandes," 2 vols., 1920–2 (trans. C. F. Atkinson, "The Decline of the West," 1926–8).

TROELTSCH, E. "Die Soziallehren der christlichen Kischen und Gruppen," 1912.

—— "Protestantism and Progress," trans. W. Montgomery, 1912.

TYLOR, E. B. "Primitive Culture," 2 vols., 1871 (4th ed., 1903).

VICO, G. B. "Principii d'una scienza nuova" (1725–30), 2 vols., 1831.

253

WEILL, G. "L'école Saint-Simonienne," 1896.
WHITEHEAD, A. N. "Science and the Modern World," 1926.
WISSLER, C. "Man and Culture," 1923.
—— "The American Indian," 2nd ed., 1922.